Face-Off *with* Dementia

How Hope and Courage
Made a Difference

By

SHIRLEY J. DIETZ

Published by hope*books
2217 Matthews Township Pkwy
Suite D302
Matthews, NC 28105
www.hopebooks.com

hope*books is a division of hope*media

Printed in the United States of America

First paperback edition.
Paperback ISBN: 979-8-89185-405-5
Hardcover ISBN: 979-8-89185-347-8
Ebook ISBN: 979-8-89185-394-2
Library of Congress Number: 2025950942

Acknowledgments

Many thanks to friends, readers of my blog, and beta readers who encouraged the writing of this book. Your patience has been astounding. Your kind questions about the progress, or lack of it, have brought me back to the manuscript time after time.

Thank you to my previous client, Scottie Stoddard, who helped me develop the skills and confidence needed to care for Dennis at home. You are no longer with us, but you are not forgotten.

Thank you, Mom, Julia, Esther, and my brothers, for all the times you listened and were kind.

And thank You to God, for all that You have taught me about love and life through this experience. It was only seeing it all from Your perspective that made it possible for Dennis and me to go through this time together with peace. Thank you for the promises You kept and those You will still keep in the future. It is my hope that You will be honored through this account.

Table of Contents

Introduction

So here I am, me and my cup of coffee, thinking about the past and attempting to explain it in writing. It has helped me a lot to have a written record of those five years of our lives when Lewy body dementia was what we lived with. It helped me as I wrote down the frustrations, fears, and events as they happened, unfiltered. But it helps now even more, keeping the details fresh in my mind, preserving precious memories of a person and an experience that will always be part of me. There were decades of life before Dennis and I had dementia on our radar, and to fully describe our journey, I will tell some of that.

I met Dennis when we were students at a small, church-based university in Texas. He had already earned a PhD in Physics at Penn State but was following his desire to grow spiritually and to find a wife who was like-minded. That's where I came in. He was 28 and I was 22 in 1973 when we married.

During our time in Texas, he taught sciences at the school where we met, and I finished a nursing degree. When the college closed, his job options included transferring to another campus in Pasadena, California, which he did. Until that point, we had hardly ever disagreed on anything, but we fought most of the way there. I did not want to live on the West Coast. It was the bicentennial year of 1976.

Thankfully, our time there was short. When we packed our trailer and climbed out of the valley of smog in 1979, neither of us was sad to go. He was leaving teaching and dreamed of his own business, helping people conserve energy and live "small but beautiful". He was years ahead of the trend. I was eight months pregnant.

We went to northern Wisconsin, where I had grown up. This was where our two children were born. There were some lean years financially while he tried one angle after another. He sold waste oil furnaces, solar systems for hot water, heat exchangers, and ventilation systems. With each one, he learned more about the physics behind the energy conservation world. It was also where he learned that he was not cut out for being self-employed. But he now had valuable experience, and he was smart. He faced the fact that in order to support his family, he would have to get a "real job".

The French company that hired him was establishing its American headquarters in Florida, so back to the South we went. He and an office manager were the only two in the beginning, and his PhD in Physics made the company look good on paper. Bradenton, on the Gulf Coast, was one of the last places either one of us had ever thought we would live. In 1987, it became home for the next thirty years.

And how he loved that job! It was the perfect blend of travel, technology, challenge, and security. He planned on dying someday at his desk, of old age. Even during summer vacations, he usually preferred to stay at home, working, where he was sure he was needed. His church activities and his favorite hobby, playing horn in the community band, were enough vacation for him.

A lot of living took place over those years. The daughters finished school and left home for college and work. It was a good life. Sure, there were occasional health concerns, but nothing that a few good supplements and blood pressure medication wouldn't fix. At least that's what he thought.

I began writing about our dementia experience in 2018, when Dennis himself began to notice changes in his health that worried him. The rest of this book is a record of things he told me and of my journal entries. It was a memorable five-year journey, a time when we grew closer to each other and, most importantly, closer to God.

Prologue: Dennis at Work

Early Summer 2018
Bradenton, Florida

Dennis shuffled down the hall to his office. He was wishing he didn't have to make quite so many trips to the bathroom and back. In the back of his mind, he shrugged it off. Like so many other things, it was probably just part of getting old.

He had started out as a sales rep thirty years ago, when the company, based in France, was new to the U.S. Air quality issues and energy conservation were finally starting to be important to the ventilation industry. He probably should have owned half the company by now if contract changes over the years hadn't kept that from happening. Even his patented inventions were owned by the company. But he was well known and valued in the ventilation industry among his peers, and that was what mattered most to him.

He loved being at work. The company had grown significantly over the time he had been there and he was the last of the original crew. He liked visiting the warehouse. The newer hires worked there, assembling and constructing components of the ventilation systems they sold. He was their friend from the front office. He was the one who knew their kids' names and didn't mind talking to them.

His office, since they had moved to a new building, was near the front entrance. It was a short distance from the reception desk, and his door was usually open. It was a small office, but had room for three chairs, a bookcase, a file cabinet, and an L-shaped desk. It had been two years since the move, but boxes that had yet to be unpacked were stacked two and three high along the only empty wall and behind the desk. They held books, papers, and magazines of his trade, some from decades earlier. He hadn't unpacked them because he seldom needed to see a piece of paper twice.

There were no pictures on the walls. The only ornaments on the desk were odd pieces of equipment that he was studying. Nothing got dusted or straightened. His office was the place where he sat and talked on the phone to people all over the country. People called about complex problems with their buildings, their heating, cooling, and ventilation issues, which he listened to and usually solved. He not only had a PhD in Physics, but also years of experience in related fields. The information people needed was usually right there in his head, requiring only a patient explanation on his part. He often had a new friend afterwards, due to his willingness to listen and chat.

He walked to his desk and pulled out the chair to sit. A frown of concern wrinkled his brow. Someone had put an adult diaper, a Depends, on it. Not good, he thought, not good. Even though it was probably a joke, he couldn't help sensing the disrespect that came along with it. It made him feel old.

***

Fastening on his helmet, he backed the E-bike out of the parking shelter. The rain had stopped an hour ago, but it could start again at a moment's notice, and he didn't want to be in it. The road could be slick. He only had two miles to travel home, but caution was always uppermost in his mind these days. He could ride a bike, but his balance was not great anymore.

He was very proud of his electric bike. It was Lee Iacocca's innovative project and was sold only at auto dealerships. It had full suspension, lights and signals, saddlebags for his briefcase - pretty much everything. It was a whole lot cheaper to operate than his truck and just right for going back and forth to the office.

Traffic was light. He was earlier than most leaving this industrial part of the city. Up ahead, a rail line, set into the pavement, crossed the road at an angle. It always made him a little skittish to go over it because of the unevenness and the gaps between the rails. This time, the front tire touched the rail and slipped to the left. He panicked and jerked the handlebars to the right.

It was over too fast for him to be sure what had transpired. He was on the pavement, the heavy bike on top of his legs. The gear shift and ignition wires were twisted loose, dangling. The rearview mirror was a few feet away and shattered. A car was coming. The pain wasn't letting him think clearly, but he knew his situation was not looking good.

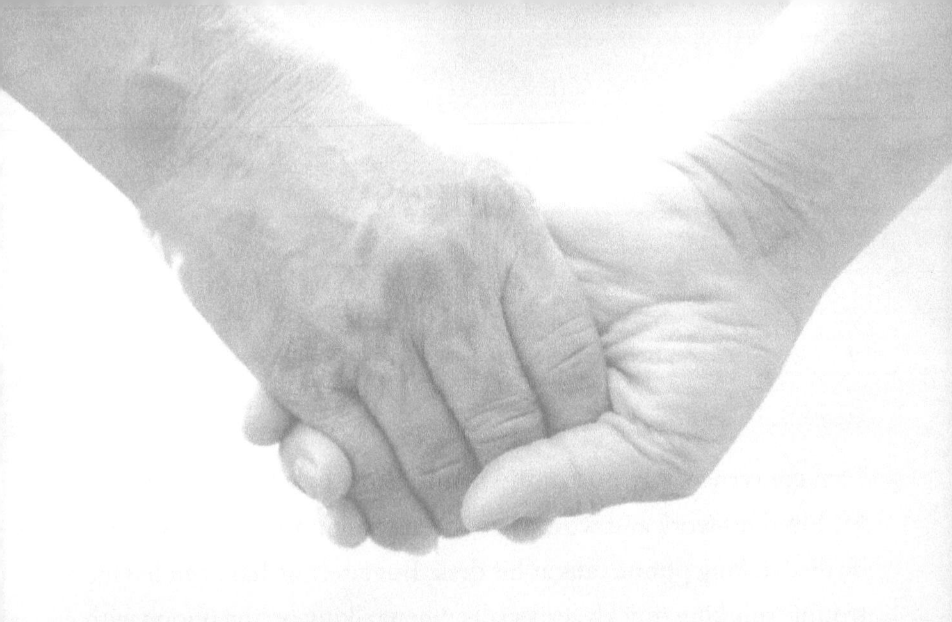

Part One: Discovery

Changes

June 1, 2018
Bradenton, FL

I am concerned. My husband, Dennis, hadn't planned on retiring. He loved his work and would have been content to work till the day he died, taking phone calls at his desk. But lately he has been having trouble thinking quickly, especially when talking on the phone with his clients. He used to have facts and figures instantly available, but not anymore.

His co-workers tell him that he walks like an old man. They make fun of him, good-naturedly, of course, but that doesn't make it feel any better. He's been passed over for promotion. He's not sure why, but they often seem to be talking behind his back. They throw trash in the back of his truck. This isn't the kind of stuff he usually tells me about work, so I know it's bothering him, a lot.

He's fallen a couple of times, too. Obstacles trip him. He had an accident and stopped riding his fancy electric bike to work. He stopped wanting to drive the car when he ran into a traffic cone and cracked the oil pan. His night vision wasn't very good and his reactions were slow. I started driving him to work, and he didn't object.

He has started to look forward to retiring, which is certainly a change. He isn't feeling well.

Our home, the OneAcreWoods, is on the market. I am working hard to pack up our things and stage the house, hoping for a quick sale. Dennis has been wrapping things up at the office. I would love it if he had the energy to be more involved with the physical work at home, but he doesn't. He falls asleep on the couch most evenings. We are both tired and ready for a change, which, I am sure, retirement will produce.

We have been planning for the last year to leave Florida. We are waiting for Dennis's retirement party at the end of the month, and then we will make the move to Wisconsin. We want to be closer to my mother, who is in her late eighties and needs our assistance. We want to be in Wisconsin by August for a family reunion, and then to settle into our new life.

Is It NPH?

June 13, 2018
Bradenton, FL

Dennis is so excited that there might be an explanation for his decline of late, and more than excited that there may be something to reverse it. He spent hours tonight watching videos of people and doctors who have dealt with symptoms like his and treated them. His two daughters, Julia and Esther, and I are used to his approach. Extensive research, reading books and articles, watching documentaries—he has to try to know everything. It's the way his brain works.

Yesterday at the doctor's office, I listened as he gave the doctor a "sort of" picture of his fatigue and discomfort. But there came a spot where I had to interrupt and tell the doctor that it was worse than what he was hearing. This man doesn't take walks anymore, sleeps whenever he's not moving, and has zero energy.

The doctor asked him a question, "Do you shuffle when you walk?" And of course, he does--like a woman nine months pregnant. Then he asked a couple of other questions, and Dennis had to tell him about his memory problems, his hypertension, and his urinary urgency. The doc said, "I think you've got NPH, normal pressure hydrocephalus." I had never heard of it.

The three outstanding symptoms that almost everyone with NPH has are the shuffle walk, the memory loss, and urinary problems, all of which are familiar to the husband. The test for it is a spinal tap.

They remove some fluid, and often the shuffle walk is gone right away. They compare the walking ability before and after to see if it improves. The treatment is brain surgery to place a permanent shunt and relieve pressure. So now our schedule is going to be full of doctor appointments to follow up on this news, as well as our ordinary health check-ups.

We don't know for sure that it's NPH, but Dennis will be really disappointed if it's not what he has. If he does have it, this is pretty important. We've been feeling scared at how rapidly things have changed for him and have been praying for answers. We thought his symptoms had more to do with his inability to lose weight, but maybe we're being shown something we had never thought of or known about. Kind of exciting, except there is also quite a risk with brain surgery.

In one way, I've been happy about how Dennis and I have worked together lately, to manage the move, the changes in health, the prospect of retirement and lower income—we have a three–way talk with God every morning about everything on our minds. Just saying that we pray doesn't adequately describe it. We put it all out there before God and each other. It has been so good for us. We don't know what the path ahead holds for us, but as long as God is marking out the way, we are not afraid to follow.

This Summer

June 23, 2018
Bradenton, Florida

It seems like we've been selling and getting ready to move for months already! We aren't gone yet, but we are close. I've had so much to do that writing has been put aside for a couple of weeks.

Dennis has been finishing up his last weeks at American Aldes Ventilation. They finally realize he is leaving and are asking him questions and scrambling to learn the things he will not be doing for them anymore. I have been driving him to work and picking him up at the end of the day.

And coming up soon is Dennis's retirement party!!! I am so excited to see the husband getting honored by his co-workers. He has been faithfully on the job for 35 years and has been through a lot with this company. They have been planning a special lunch out at a restaurant and a surprise. I have no idea what it is.

Meanwhile, at home, I have been emptying out closets, dressers, cupboards, and the garage, and packing everything in boxes and bags. About half of it all was put in a container from Pack Rat and is now in a warehouse in Tampa. I've also been trying to use up our food supply, hoping that we don't have another hurricane before we move. I sold the freezer, and the garage is looking empty.

It's hard to do these things without making messes, but I've had to keep the house ready to show in case an interested buyer comes our way. That has included keeping the yard mowed, weeds pulled, and trees trimmed. We've had two open houses, both of which had zero visitors. Really. Everyone is up North, I guess.

It was bittersweet for me, but I sold my car, my beloved Mazda. We also traded Dennis's red truck for a used, but newer model, Chevy Colorado, in a sophisticated grey. And knowing we would be taking a lot of things with us to Wisconsin, I ordered a topper to go with the new-to-us truck. It will take weeks to make and getting it put on will probably be the last thing before we leave. I still have to find and buy a small trailer to hold the things we want to take north with us. I'm learning things about trailers, axles, sway bars and more that I didn't know I would be learning.

Last but not least, we are trying to keep as healthy as possible in this busy stage. Moving means starting over with new healthcare providers, too, so we are both doing our last visits to doctors and dentists, compiling our health records to take north with us. Dennis has been very frustrated and depressed lately with some of his symptoms, but we know it's best to wait until we have moved to address them. I need to make an appointment at Mayo Clinic in Minnesota for him. I'm concerned about whether they will accept him and what the timeline would be.

I've been planning our trip to Wisconsin, via Greensboro, to see our daughter Julia. We will probably spend a few days with her, but we absolutely have to be finished traveling and in Wisconsin by the end of July. The first week in August is the Smith Family Reunion and we are going to be there helping it happen!

So, a lot has been happening, even as some important things, like the sale of the house, have not been happening. We are learning and practicing our waiting skills. And since it doesn't make much difference where we wait, we will do it with family in Wisconsin. We are not discouraged. The house will sell eventually.

He Is Retiring!

June 27, 2018
Bradenton, Florida

I'm overwhelmed. It is the night before the husband's retirement celebration and I am nervously trying to think through all his medical concerns. I know I will be asked tomorrow about how he is faring and what news we have. It is complicated.

Our doctors here advised that Dennis should be seen for diagnosis at Mayo Clinic in Rochester, Minnesota. If he has NPH, he will need the specialists they have there. My head is swimming from being on the internet all evening looking at sleep apnea home tests and CPAP machines and applications for an appointment at the Clinic. I don't even want to figure out how these things are going to fit into the next two weeks before we head out. It's too much.

Both daughters have their tickets for the family reunion in Wisconsin in August. People are posting their plans to attend. I am just hoping we will be there and not in a hospital somewhere. We talk daily with my mom, and I can tell she is a bit skeptical and wonders if we can pull this off. I'm trusting that my Master Planner has it all figured out, and I'm going to be okay with the circumstances as he arranges them. I think I appear calm, generally, but the fact that I keep going to the refrigerator is evidence of what is under the surface. I'm feeding my anxiety. Food doesn't exactly help how I feel, but I crave it anyway.

There doesn't seem to be much time between trips these days. Trips taking the husband to work, trips to the doctor's office, trips to Goodwill, trips to the store. The good thing about having only one vehicle is that the husband and I are together a lot, coming and going places. We are talking in a different way, or rather, about different things than usual. Instead of him talking about his work with fans and ventilation (thumbs down in my book), we talk about how he feels about retirement and the preparations for moving and other stuff I find interesting and necessary. This is a good thing.

Trucks and Trailers

7/16/ 2018
Bradenton, Florida

Trucks and trailers. I've had enough of them, but I dare not complain because there is more to come and I depend upon them. They are a part of moving. Graceful acceptance is in order. Fortunately, I like our new truck a lot.

The other truck in my life is the one that brings and takes away my PackRat container. It has been in our yard, struggling to turn around and get in position, four separate times now. The last time was last week, when the fully loaded container left on its way to North Carolina. I had been packing it for three days and it was full. According to instructions, I was not to exceed 6,000 pounds, but it had been a long time since I had weighed any of my furniture or belongings. Who does that?

As I shoved the last heavy box of flatware over into a recliner, stuck high on a pile of book boxes and marble slabs, I had a bad feeling about the weight. I shut and bolted the door anyway because the driver had called and was only five minutes away from picking it up.

I innocently asked the driver how they weighed the containers, and he pointed to a scale gauge on the lift. His words, "We've been taking a lot of overweight loads lately, but the limit is 8,000 pounds, because the lift can't handle more than that." Honestly, I went inside to pray while he hooked it up and took the container up a few feet.

God was listening. It was 8,000 pounds, and he gave me a thumbs-up and took it away. I'm still marveling.

Because I am not at all superstitious, Friday the 13th of July will be our departure date. We will set out in our grey Chevy Colorado with a new 6x12-foot single-axle trailer behind it. We have been given some guidelines in gauging the weight of this trailer, too, which I've forgotten. Hope it won't be too heavy.

On the Way

July 18, 2018
Gibsonville, NC

We made it to North Carolina! Several large items in the trailer were for my daughter Julia, who lives near Greensboro, so the day after arriving, I unpacked the trailer. With Julie's help, we reorganized and reloaded my trailer and then unloaded and reorganized her storage trailer. She is even more of a truck and trailer girl than I am. Her trailer is twice the size of mine, and so is her truck, but she has an excuse. She is an equine veterinarian and needs big equipment.

What remains for us (me, the husband, the truck, and trailer) is the 18 hours of driving to our destination in Wisconsin. Gonna be such fun, right? We are going to be very familiar with each other by the time we're done.

Introspection

July 21, 2018
Hayward, Wisconsin

The world has gone a bit surreal, and I'm not quite sure where to place myself in it. Thirty-one years ago, I left Hayward, Wisconsin for life in Florida. It was a completely new life in every way. Now I am back in Wisconsin, but again it is a new life in nearly every way. The actual "work" of moving is done, so now I have time to think about what has happened. I'm finding introspection to be a mixed blessing.

We arrived last night after a long drive, suitcases in tow, with plans to catch up with family members and visit childhood haunts. The surreal part is that we won't be packing up again in two weeks for the trip back to Florida. We will stay here and see the seasons change, make new friends, start new routines, and settle in. Instead of calling Mom every morning, I will meet her in the kitchen as we get our first cup of coffee. Instead of cleaning my own house and taking care of the Florida "Oneacrewoods," I will be looking for ways to help others with their homes and yards.

For months, this change from one life to another has seemed so far off and so slow in coming that it was hard to believe it would happen at all. "If you ever get here," Mom would say. I would reassure her that the challenge of the week would be met and that we were making progress. But honestly, I had moments when I cried and felt like

I couldn't do it. The most valuable thing I learned from it all is that I should not spend a lot of time looking at the large picture. It can be too daunting to view as a whole. One day, one step at a time is all that I was designed for. Each small accomplishment should get its full measure of satisfaction and celebration. One by one, the hurdles got crossed, and now I am sitting at the end of the course wondering how I got here. Once again, the passage of time has created a miracle, a change.

I learned about home improvement, about hiring painters and contractors and overseeing projects. I learned about getting medical and financial records in place and ready for a move. I learned about selling and buying trucks and what goes into the making of a good trailer. I learned I had friends. I learned that hard things become easier when I pray about them and decide to trust I've been heard. I learned that some things must be waited for and are beyond my control. I learned that having even one concrete task that I can do is a comfort and a blessing. Get busy and do it, then look for the next thing.

The house in Florida has not sold yet. We joke around, saying we are homeless, because the house is empty and our things are in storage. Instead, I'm going to remember that my goal was to be with more of my family, and that has happened. If home is where my people are, I'm not homeless. Instead, I've come home.

I'm thinking ahead to the medical appointment at Mayo Clinic. I'm glad to be closer to my family, because I think we will need the support.

We Move In

August 30,2018
Hayward, Wisconsin

August has been so busy. Dennis and I had a week to unpack and move into Mom's condo with her. We are a bit crowded in the small guest room. Dennis has the closet for his things, but my clothes are in the garage closet, as weird as that sounds.

And then we were into the family reunion. It was so much fun and so exhausting.

It's taken nearly the whole month of August to get our legal life transferred to this new state. Vehicle registration, vehicle insurance, medical insurance, and address updates to every account we've ever had have taken so many phone calls and hours on the computer. And the most important business was arranging the details for the upcoming trip. We've waited a long time for the appointment at Mayo, and we really want to get some answers.

Going to Mayo

September 9, 2018
La Crosse, Wisconsin

We are on the way to Mayo Clinic in Minnesota. It's rather famous for its research and careful medical analysis. The three of us, Mom, Dennis, and I, are headed to Rochester, hoping to find answers. Some days, the husband feels like he is losing his mind, and he has been very happy to let me organize our trip. I've tried to make sure everything is in order for him to have a good, thorough appointment.

We've had unpleasant, last-minute surprises about insurance coverage. What I thought would be three days, maybe four, of testing is now stretching out over a week. We may go home for the weekend and back on Monday rather than live in a motel the whole time. I just have uncertainty about whether we are prepared. The husband has not been able to help at all, really.

But we are not fearful. We will do all we can think of to do, even though it is clear that we are not in control here. We haven't found any other person who is either. That still leaves us with God, and He has done some pretty cool things. We've depended on Him before and can't say we've ever been sorry. I'm going with whatever He sets up. Whatever happens, we'll claim it's good because He says it will be. There's no reason to think He would lie about that.

Mayo Clinic Day 1

September 11, 2018
Rochester, Minnesota

Right away, let me say that if you have to get sick, this is a really good place to go.

We left my brother's home near La Crosse early this morning, and in a little over an hour, we were in Rochester, MN. The clinic and its hospitals are the focal point of this small city, and it is fairly easy to navigate. There are people in every parking lot and in every lobby waiting to answer questions for newcomers like us. They are used to doing it, and because they have developed good systems, things went smoothly for us.

I was amazed that we drove to the 9th floor (top) of the parking garage and headed back down again before we found an empty spot, and at such an early hour! There were rows of sturdy wheelchairs at curbside for anyone not inclined to walk and good signage that was easy to follow. This stuff is so important! Knowing where to park and where to go for appointments was one of my main concerns.

There were no long lines and no extended waiting periods! We might run into this later on, but today was extraordinarily good in that respect. After check-in, we were helped by an appointment specialist, Mr. Smith, and put into an exam room to wait for our doctor, Dr. Jones. "Smith and Jones" jokes were exchanged.

Dr. Jones got a detailed report from Dennis. He seemed to be a good listener and made notes as we went along through the exam. He wasn't a white lab coat doctor, which I thought was interesting. He had a nice, expensive-looking tweed suit, longish, curly, dark hair, and a trimmed beard. He gave Dennis quite a few tests as he talked with him, and at the end announced that he had mild cognitive impairment, maybe borderline dementia. We knew that, but it was nice to have it verified. He is in favor of finding out why. Not too long after that evaluation, the husband had a brain MRI, with and without scary-sounding contrast medium. Very nice professionals conducted this testing with hardly any wait time. Mom and I got a light lunch while this was going on. We were done and on our way to a motel before 3 pm. The accommodations here are clean, comfortable, and quite adequate.

We rested, had a "comfort" dinner at Olive Garden, and were back in our motel, ready to get to sleep early. Dennis was supposed to have a PET scan tomorrow, but because it has not yet been authorized, it is postponed until Thursday afternoon. I'm hoping the insurance will cover it, because Dr. Jones said it was probably the most definitive test and will show whether he has normal pressure hydrocephalus (NPH), Alzheimer's disease (AD), or Lewy body dementia (LBD). We need to get authorized for this scan, and that is what we are praying for tonight.

The lumbar puncture will take place Thursday morning. The neuro psych evaluation was scheduled for next Monday, but we are hoping for cancellations so we can get it done this week. It's a nice enough motel, but not where we want to live for that long.

The doctor also wants Dennis to get another sleep study and an ophthalmology work-up. Those can be done later in October—we will come back for them.

So, it's been a good day, as well as can be hoped for. We are in fairly good spirits.

Mayo Clinic Day 2

September 12, 2018
Rochester, MN

I am beginning to know my way around, where the different buildings are, where to pick up the shuttle, where to go to eat. The husband is getting better at it, too, but he doesn't go anywhere alone and likes to have someone to follow.

Our appointments were not scheduled the way we would have wished, but we were told it was possible to change some of them. The schedulers told us, "Be a checker!" and wrote it on our instruction sheet. I had to ask what that meant. It's their suggestion that you be on hand for the test you want to get, in case someone cancels. It's like standby status at the airport. We were on hand at 7 am and 12 pm, the designated times, with no success.

After our morning wait, we went down to the business office and asked about our insurance authorization for the needed PET scan. It was not a busy place, and a very competent person helped us right away. She made some calls and told me that Dr. Jones's report had been sent to the insurance company. I will call tomorrow morning and see if it has had any effect.

Going back and forth as many times as we did gave us some good experience riding the shuttle. It is easier and cheaper than driving and will be our main mode of transportation. There has been free time between some appointments, but we are finding ourselves very easy to entertain. We shop at Walmart, take naps, read, and watch TV to fill our time away from the clinic. The highlight of each day is dinner at a restaurant. Tonight's choice was Outback.

I am trying to resurrect memories of my year in Rochester while in nursing school. A lot has changed, but I was relieved to find one place was much the same. Silver Lake Park was still there. The lake itself was part of the Zumbro River and there was a power plant connected with it. Because the water was warmed by the power plant, it didn't freeze as quickly as other bodies of water in the area. It was home to great multitudes of Canadian geese all year round and quite a sight to see. I remember times when it was cold enough to warrant goose rescue attempts for those animals that were getting frozen into the ice. The geese are still there, along with a sign asking people not to feed them. A large goose produces three pounds of poop per day, and all that creates a significant bacteria problem for the lake. We read the signs with all this information, and for a few moments, we didn't think about why we were in Rochester, Minnesota. It was nice.

Tomorrow we will be on standby for the neuro-psych evaluation again, and hopefully will get time to visit my Aunt Evelyn in the afternoon. We are all a little worried about our daughter, Julia. Hurricane Florence is heading toward North Carolina, and Greensboro is in the center of the all-important cone of possibility. We know what hurricanes are like! This world is full of things we can't control. How plain that is.

Mayo Clinic Day 3

September 12, 2018
Rochester, Minnesota

I am about ready to tear my hair out and be taken to the asylum in a straitjacket. I've been talking to my insurance company.

Me: Yes, hello. I'm calling to check on an authorization for a PET scan for my husband, Dennis. Where do we stand on this request?

Insurance rep: I can check on that for you, just a moment... I don't see a request for a PET scan in the notes. I see four other authorizations, blah, blah, blah...

Me: Mayo Clinic sent our doctor's notes to you yesterday, and they were told the decision was pending. It's an out-of-network issue, and it's complicated. Do you have someone who handles these cases that I can talk to? (I give them a case number and the history of the last five days of phone calls.)

Insurance rep: No, I can't say that we do, and the notes we have don't mention a PET scan at all. (She tries to find more information but comes back with the same answer.)

Me: (Calling Mayo Clinic business desk in a panic.) I've just called my insurance to check on the authorization, as you suggested, and they don't know anything about a request for a PET scan. It's supposed to happen tomorrow. What can I do?

Clinic rep: We called your insurance at 8 am this morning to see if the authorization was given. They did get our fax yesterday about the doctor's evaluation, and the matter is still pending. We should know something today.

Me: Why are they not able to find this anywhere in his record? They have the other authorizations, but nothing for the PET scan. They say they don't even have case numbers like the one I was told to give them.

Clinic rep: (explaining all kinds of stuff about a special review board for out of network authorizations) We gave them the doctor's recommendations and I'm sure they will be getting back to us. Don't worry, we have all day today and most of tomorrow to work this out. It will get resolved.

So I called the insurance company again, got a different rep who said basically the same thing, with the added information that she had never heard of a special review board and said she would know if there was one. I made sure she knew that this was getting very mysterious and confusing to get two completely conflicting stories about the status of the request. She assured me they did not have a request recorded, but I could get one started. She told me how.

I didn't want to call the clinic again, but I did. No surprises there—the same report. At least everyone is consistent. I guessed it was up to me. Which story did I want to believe? So, I went with the clinic, and am praying that they were right. I really did not want to make any more calls. Tomorrow, we will find out if that was a good decision.

A bright spot in the day came when we got a call mid-morning that we were no longer on standby for the neuro-psych evaluation. We have an appointment for 7 am tomorrow! They also rescheduled the lumbar puncture for Friday morning. After one more meeting with Dr. Jones, we will be done. We are going home on Friday!

But we will probably be coming back in a month or so. Whatever. Maybe by then we will have new insurance, the kind that's not so special that no one knows about it.

Mayo Clinic Day 4

September 13, 2018
Rochester, Minnesota

Our fourth day at Mayo Clinic has had its ups and downs, but it was also the day with the most accomplishments.

We started early, the third day in a row that we were up, fed, and on the bus shortly after 7. Soon after arriving, Dennis was met by the professional doing his testing and disappeared for a couple hours. He came out for a quick snack and then went back for another two hours. I thought for sure he would be exhausted by then. I was called back for a brief discussion with him and one of the doctors, and then we rode the bus back to the motel.

While the husband was getting tested this morning, I made a trip to the business office to check on the infamous pre-authorization request for the PET scan (still pending) and then wandered around. There was so much stunning artwork on the walls, and every window gave a different view of the city outside. The main lobby had walls of glass with marble and granite floors and staircases. Visitors would sit down at the grand piano and play a tune while people of all ages and cultures walked past. Watching people stirs me to wonder what is going on in their lives that they are here, probably searching for answers like we are.

To give Dennis time for a nap, we decided to take the car to the next test instead of riding the bus. The PET scan was scheduled for 4:50, and Dennis would be fasting until it was over. We knew he would need to eat soon after, so Mom came along with us and we planned to go right to a restaurant afterwards.

Every time I checked on the request for authorization, the answer was the same. At 4:30 it was still pending and no one could figure out the persistent problem or get satisfactory answers. It was the most expensive test but the most important, so we paid for it, out of pocket, to make sure he was able to take it. Insurance will get billed, but we have no clue whether or not they will pay anything on it. I'm thankful for a credit card that allows that kind of expense.

Mom and I read our books and waited while Dennis had his head scanned. The books we're working on are both very riveting and we wouldn't have minded waiting a little longer. As it was, the test was over quickly and we were off to have supper at The Porch, a converted railroad station, now a family-style restaurant.

Tomorrow will wind up the Mayo experience for this time. One test remains, the lumbar tap. I don't know if I'm excited about this one or not. It's the most invasive and has a bit more risk to it, but is also one that the husband thinks could make a difference in some of his symptoms. It's at 9 am. All that remains after that is the meeting with our primary specialist, Dr. Jones, at 3 pm. It is expected that he will have results from everything to discuss with us. I am used to waiting a long time to be told results, so I will be surprised if it happens. We will drive home immediately after that.

There is something we all think about as we watch the crowds of people at the clinic, on the bus, and in the waiting rooms. All these people are living out their private battles with illnesses that have befallen them and changed their lives. Things are not normal anymore for them. They all have stories. They all wonder what their future will hold. We are not alone by any means.

A Diagnosis

September 15, 2018
Hayward, Wisconsin

We've had a little over 24 hours now to sit with the weight of the doctor's words, process them, and test how our involuntary reactions are stacking up. He didn't tell us what we wanted to hear most, that the husband's problems could be fixed with surgery. It wasn't NPH. It was, or is, a form of dementia called Lewy body dementia. It feels like a death sentence.

Even though this is the second most common form of dementia, right behind Alzheimer's, it is not high on the public awareness scale. Everything has an acronym, so LBD is what it's called. There is research, there are educational resources, there are support groups, but no cure as of yet. It's not something anyone wants to experience.

The doctor spent time explaining thoroughly how he arrived at the diagnosis. He told us exactly how he wanted to treat the symptoms and what things should be done as far as lifestyle changes. We were already doing many of them, so life will not change greatly for us. There are a couple of new medications and a few new cautions. Not much is different, except now we know.

We are going to be okay. The husband is okay. He likes telling people it hasn't affected his sense of humor at all, and I always agree. It is as bad as it always has been. He is still very much himself, as most of his friends know. At Mayo, he did quite well on his cognitive tests, and he will discuss complex things at times and have no trouble at all. I would say that he is more emotional, more compassionate and understanding of others. He is more grateful and aware than in the past. It's simply because life has given him a jolt that enables him to see pain and struggles in the lives of those around him. I think he feels held and loved by God more because he needs it more.

He is looking for any way that God might be able to use him. You know how men are (well, a lot of them anyway). They want to feel useful and not dependent. He wants to share his story and encourage others. He wants to call himself the "Demented Disciple" (not my idea). We'll see how that works out. It is, however, going to be an experience that we go through together as a family. I know I will have to write about it, as a caregiver, in order to stay mentally, emotionally, and spiritually healthy. I don't think it's going to be easy.

The tests yesterday at Mayo were interesting. I may write more about them when I feel more in the mood to inform. The ride home was pleasant, and we were glad to get to Hayward around 9 pm. That's it for tonight.

Thinking It Over

September 17, 2018
Hayward, Wisconsin

Now September is more than half over. As often happens when a large, mind-consuming task is done, I'm left wondering what to do next. All the things that I haven't thought about while concentrating on our trip to Mayo Clinic are probably still there needing to be attended to, but I'm not sure I'm remembering them all. That is my most frequent prayer, that I would be reminded to do things at the right time and that nothing would fall through the cracks. Things that do fall through the cracks, unnoticed, create bigger problems later.

We are becoming a little more devoted to our keto eating plan now that the husband is motivated to protect his brain cells, keep those mitochondria healthy and all. It is a good diet for neurodegenerative conditions, as well as cancer, diabetes, and heart issues. Since we've been telling people about Dennis's diagnosis, I have received lots of suggestions of things to try and things to avoid. We already know about some of them, but will probably try them all eventually. None are ridiculous. They all have associated success stories.

Which brings me to the point of how different this disease can be from one person to the next. Each individual paves their own unique way down this path. There are some common traits, but even those come and go. While it is interesting and hope-producing to read stories of cures and great improvements, it can be equally devastating to read about unsuccessful outcomes. I would rather think that the husband's story is his own and it's not been told yet. Let's just live well and watch what unfolds. Circumstances are troubling, but God pays no attention to circumstances, since they do not control Him in any way. It only makes sense to us to trust God and try to think like He does. We can do this.

I am so grateful for all our friends who have responded lovingly, given us encouraging words, and have let us know that they are praying for us. A health threat is a bad reason to be drawing attention, but because of it, we are newly aware of people out there who care. I think that we could relieve people's fears for us if they could be around Dennis for a while. I think they would be reassured that he is still himself and thinking well.

Tomorrow we are making a fun trip to the nearest big city, Duluth, Minnesota. We are seeing some friends and then going to my favorite department store, Sam's Club (lame, but true). We are looking forward to it. Life is good. We are not downcast. But I hope all those friends don't stop praying for us. Just sayin'...

PART TWO: OUR NEW LIFE

Finances

October 12, 2018
Hayward, Wisconsin

Today we will go to a financial advisor.

It's not that we have great stores of wealth to manage, but we have tried to be smart with what the husband has earned in his many years of service. And now that we will need to pay for expensive health-care, we would rather not rely on others to support us. Given how quickly money can disappear these days, it is good to have advice. And is it really money, or is it just numbers on digital screens? It's a strange world.

With me, it gets stranger still. I am not an astute financier. The thought of me managing any amount of money is not a good thought. I am in awe of CPAs and financial advisors, even of bank tellers. But I have to do what I can, now that the husband gets too tired when he thinks about numbers. God helps me. Oh, and I have this. I have advisors.

What people like me need to do, I think, is find and hire others who have the gift. The IRS is my enemy at present, so we have hired our own army of money soldiers. They are mercenaries from some other planet, judging by the language they speak. I don't understand most of what they say. They seem friendly.

As I said, the bottom line is that God helps me. I just ask Him that none of my mistakes be fatal, and that there will always be a roof over our heads and beans and rice to eat. So far, He has greatly exceeded my requests. I am grateful. And I am amazed at how many interesting things I can learn along the way. There is a website for every financial account, of course, and a password or two for each portal. There are secret questions and chosen pictures to keep me from wandering into the dark web, whatever that is. All I have to do is keep my memory intact. I am hoping that won't be a problem.

So, I am praying today for my soon-to-be financial advisor and putting him in God's hands. It will be okay. We will be okay. The stock market goes down, the economy collapses, but we will still be okay.

The Elephant

October 16, 2018
Hayward, Wisconsin

Part of my problem as a writer is that I often feel like a minor player in someone else's drama. The really hard things are happening to Dennis, and so much of it is his story. Even if he doesn't get around to writing his own story, I feel like I'm stealing if I write about it. I probably would not tell it the way he would. Would I get it right?

In searching for reasons why he was diagnosed with Lewy body dementia just weeks after his retirement, the husband has wondered if he is supposed to share his experience with others. Could it be he is meant to encourage others in some way, even though he is pretty sick about this whole thing? He actually says he might start a blog or write stuff down as he thinks of it. For several reasons, I think the chances of him writing anything are slim. For one, he has a history of brilliant ideas that never see action. I don't see his diagnosis changing that.

Reason two, he doesn't have experience expressing feelings. He has them, but they don't usually bother him or beg to be shared. He would like to share things now, but they end up coming out in long, convoluted histories of his life journey, accompanied by tears and a tone of desperation and sadness. He's doing it a little better now, but the first couple of weeks were tough. Any compassionate person who had time to listen patiently ended up crying with him and giving him a hug.

Reason three is simply that writing is work, and work isn't something he's looking for. Too much mental work makes his head spin.

It's true that my story has a lot to do with his story but, of course, I tell it from a very different perspective. He reads what I write. I wonder if I will be able to write what I really think, or will I change the narrative because of the effect it might have on him?

Interestingly, the two things that have helped the husband and I know each other better in the last few years are our "together" prayers and my online journal. In each place I tend to be more open, truthful, and informative. In each instance, he feels less threatened by my words because they aren't spoken directly to him; they are conversations with God or my readers. He listens better. And the same goes for him when it comes to telling God his thoughts and concerns—he might as well be honest. When he prays, I learn things about him that he doesn't think to tell me.

It certainly isn't that I don't want him to write his own story from his own perspective. I do. But not writing about this part of my own life has been hard. The vague feeling that I shouldn't, or couldn't, write about this big thing happening to us has made me not write much at all about anything. Somehow, when there is an "elephant" in the room, so to speak, writing about anything else takes second place to wondering about the elephant and what it's going to do next.

That elephant is on my mind most of the time. I might as well write about it. Probably have to.

Our New LBD Normal

November 5, 2018
Hayward, Wisconsin

This new normal—I don't really know if it can be called normal. Normal seems to mean that something stays the same over a period of time, long enough that you can grow used to it. We can't seem to grow used to things that are changing all the time as we deal with the husband's problems. "Normal" has come to mean regular frustration as he deals with less of almost everything he needs in every situation.

It snowed yesterday and was wet, slushy, and slippery everywhere we went. The husband's shoes were getting wet and were clearly not what he would need for winter, so today we shopped for boots. This is something we both remember him doing by himself, but since he no longer drives, I am with him everywhere he goes.

The first thing we had to do in the shoe department was find a place to sit down. Dennis can't walk very far or stand very long without getting tired, and he always has to sit to put on his shoes. We struggled. Putting on boots can be such hard work. I fetched pair after pair from the shelves, opened them up, and pulled and pushed until he could get his foot down inside. Each time he had to stand and test out the feel of the boot. Up and down, over and over. He was worried about the small bench he was on, as it would start to tip as he pushed himself up. We finally found a pair. I think he would have liked to go home at that point, but he had also wanted to get a new watch.

After pointing him in the direction of the jewelry counter, I thought, briefly, that I would let him look over the options and choose. But no, I decided it would be easier if I helped him, so we went together. His vision is one area where "less" keeps happening. In order to see the time, he decided the face of the watch had to be white, with dark hands and numbers that were easy to read. No shiny reflective surfaces would be suitable. The band had to be easy to close. He would have liked one that showed the date, but finally decided that he would do without since he couldn't read those small letters anyway. It didn't take us very long to pick one out, but by then he was really tired. He went to the pharmacy, where they have benches, and sat waiting while I got a few groceries.

And we are getting very good at finding restrooms in all the places we go. This was Walmart, and he had to walk to the far end of the store for that before we could leave. He walks very carefully and very slowly.

Often we think of dementia as robbing a person of their memory first. That is not a given with Lewy body dementia. Right now, some of the husband's most frustrating symptoms are motor-related. He has less strength, less balance, less flexibility, less stamina. He will tell you that he is also forgetful, but I find that he can make himself remember most anything he wants to, given enough time. He may get overwhelmed with thinking too hard, but he still thinks correctly. He remembers. And that is what is hard—remembering what he used to be able to do, but no longer can.

We got the boots. He wore them once and said they were too heavy. He could hardly lift his feet.

Mealtime Meltdown

December 3, 2018
Hayward, Wisconsin

I have been writing and fighting with computer problems all afternoon, and it has left me in a poor mood. At least that is what I'm going to blame it on.

Mealtime meltdown, and I'm not referring to some three-year-old who doesn't want to eat his broccoli. It's me. I'm at war with the idea of fixing food to eat. Although I like eating as a rule, and probably eat more than a lot of other people, I'm starting to harbor a great dislike for planning meals and cooking them. It's work. Repetitive work. Often unrewarding work. A lot of the time, I view cooking and eating as annoying interruptions.

To make matters worse, these days, when we're battling this disease, almost all food is suspect. It either causes cancer, kills off our beneficial bacteria, or is loaded with hormones or environmental poisons. We have to eat keto, organic, gluten-free, free-range everything. We have to eat our food in a 6-hour time window, drink enough water to float a boat, and avoid comfort food in general (and bread in specific). We are bombarded with messages like "food is medicine," and at the same time, we are sold a zillion supplements and told to ask our doctors for prescription meds for everything from depression to skin problems. I don't want to stop eating, but I often don't want to stop what I'm doing in order to plan and prepare food.

This afternoon, Dennis came to me as I was deep into a writing project and said, "What did you have for lunch?" What he really meant was, "What can I have for lunch?" It's evidently less demanding if he asks it that way, which he often does. We had eaten a late breakfast, and I was not ready to stop working, but I dished up a cup of soup because he was hungry. I probably should have felt more compassion for him, but I was annoyed. I had just started writing a blog post for my brother's business site, and my creative energy, which was already faltering, disappeared completely with the interruption.

Getting back to my writing, I eased my conscience with the plan to have an early dinner. A couple of hours later, I was aware that it was time to go to the kitchen, but still didn't want to leave my project and couldn't think of anything good to fix for dinner.

I went into Mom's room to see if she wanted to eat with us. Mom is in her eighties, and part of the reason for us living in Hayward with her was for me to help her with meals, but that has not happened. It's often the other way around. She has pretty much given up on our schedule and the way the husband and I try to eat. She had already stuffed herself (her words) with a taco salad not too long before, but that gave me the idea of what I could make for Dennis and myself.

So, I warmed, chopped, sprinkled, arranged—all those annoying little activities—to produce our salads and called the husband to eat. "I'll take about a third of that," he said. "You can put the rest of it away for later. I just ate soup and a sandwich."

Okay, that is my frustration—I stopped doing something I really wanted to do and stood in the kitchen fixing food for someone who now doesn't want it. I am constantly vacillating between guilt (I don't have anything ready to eat), frustration (I made food and he doesn't want any), and rage (leave me alone and let me write!).

I will admit, it's not easy living with me in charge of food. I am prone to disregarding my stomach. I can tolerate the same menu day after day. I can eat water for food, or take a walk and skip the meal altogether. I love doing so many other things more than worrying about what to eat. When it comes to food, I'm making a new plan. I'm going to cultivate friends who love to cook and will invite us to eat with them. I might also try to be a little more grown-up and do a better job of planning mealtimes. Maybe.

Anniversary Eve

January 13, 2019
Eau Claire, Wisconsin

It is anniversary eve, and tomorrow afternoon, we will have been married for 46 years. What an eventful year this has been, with retirement for the husband, an interstate move, and our house going up for sale, and then his diagnosis of Lewy body dementia.

We may have many more anniversaries, or we may not. But however many there are, we have this one to look forward to. We have an appointment with a lawyer in a nearby city to discuss estate planning. As long as we are there, it will be nice to stay in a hotel and not have to make the two-hour drive home. As long as we are staying for the night, we are going to dinner at a nice steakhouse as a celebration. I have planned it all, and it will be more of a "night away" than we have had for a long time. We need a little celebrating.

It will mark another occasion as well. Today, we got the first real paper offer on our home in Florida. It's been over six months on the market and this is the first offer we have had. It's been a hard sell because it's not just one home, it's two homes on one property. And the homes are connected. We listed it as a multi-generational property. It is the kind of buyer we had been hoping for, a young family of four and the grandparents. Their offer is a little low, but we are hoping to come to an agreement with them. In a little over a month, we could possibly be closing the sale. I have been looking forward to this for so long! It would solve several other problems as well if this could come to closing. We are praying for that.

The husband has not been feeling well, but he is pretty certain he will feel better tomorrow. Don't ask me how he knows. It's as much a spiritual and emotional matter as it is physical. The physical part is the discipline to keep to the diet he wants to be on. I am hoping the restaurant will have at least one good keto meal to choose from so he can enjoy the evening. I chose a hotel that has no stairs to climb and a nice hot tub to soak in. That should also be a treat, if he has the energy for it.

Things do fall into place at some point. Maybe this is it, if the house sells. I know we could yet be disappointed, but I'm taking care not to find out until after our anniversary. Congratulations to us. We are in it for the long haul.

A Wakeful Night

February 20, 2019
Hayward, Wisconsin

Yesterday, the day of the husband's doctor appointment, I wanted to encourage him not to be weird, not to ask the doctor to read his reams of research printouts, not to tell stories about Jimmy and Rosalynn (the Carters), not to talk about his wonderful brother who takes him seriously, and the list goes on...

But when I sat down hoping to have this conversation with him, he was all about his difficult night in which he lay awake from 10 pm to 3 am, hearing from God that it was his time to write a book and share the secrets that have been revealed to him. The secrets are mostly about magnesium. He has already decided on the title, "Wake Up and Smell the Peanut Butter."

We did have a good talk, and we prayed about the doctor appointment and about the book. I find myself again wishing he would write about his experience. That he would write a book is not a crazy idea, and it would be an interesting book, but the challenges would make it difficult.

I ended up suggesting that he dictate his writing. I offered to edit it for him. He had wanted to ask that, but was dramatically grateful that I offered before he had to ask. He also asked that I co-write his book, telling the story from my point of view, like Jimmy and Rosalynn did. He said that was God's idea, too. And because he was feeling so inspired by his dream, and so sure of God's direction on the subject of magnesium, he emailed Linda Ronstadt to tell her the problem with her voice going away was because of magnesium deficiency.

He doesn't know Linda Ronstadt. How did he ever get an email address for her? Amazing.

We Go to a Summit

March 5, 2019
Rochester, Minnesota

We have spent a couple of days at a conference, a summit on Lewy body dementia put on by Mayo Clinic. They put on a very efficient and informative event, and I'm glad we were able to go. Dennis met and talked with quite a few people who are struggling with LBD like he is, and I know it helped him to not feel alone. He viewed himself as being able to encourage others and give them hope.

I also met caregivers going through the same thing I am and much worse. It was also interesting to learn more about this complex and difficult condition. Interestingly, the only time nutrition was referenced was when they announced breakfast, lunch, and snacks (which, by the way, were very well done and worth the $30 per person registration). I'm pretty sure Dennis was the only person who said the word magnesium, and thankfully, he didn't say it very often.

This trip has been interesting in that I see how much care Dennis needs in unfamiliar environments. There is nothing about our travel that he plans or gives thought to. He tries at the last minute to be the man in charge. He asks how much gas is in the vehicle, or if I have all the cords and device chargers packed.

I appreciate our handicap vehicle tag at restaurants and stores, but sometimes it is even easier (or required) that I drop him off at the door of a place and then go park somewhere away and walk back carrying whatever stuff we have with us. It is often easier to provide him with food or drink than witness his confusion about how to get it himself. For my own sake, I take more time to look him over, making sure his clothes don't have spots on them and he doesn't have food on his face. He doesn't know how he looks in his stocking cap and puts it on in all sorts of weird ways.

It is partly for my own benefit that I try to get him to be clean-shaven and appropriately dressed, but also to keep others from forming negative first impressions. It's not all about the LBD, I don't think. He's been unaware, in varying degrees, for years and years. Or maybe it has been LBD and he's just had it longer than we know.

He takes all this herding around in good humor and jokes about it. He doesn't fight my planning and decisions, because I don't tell him ahead of time. As long as I let him think about where he wants to eat, he's good with things and enjoys himself.

His biggest challenge is finding restrooms when he needs them. We are constantly dealing with changing conditions, whether it be constipation, diarrhea, or urinary frequency, so I keep my brain noting the location of any restroom we pass by.

One concept that was presented at the conference that I find especially intriguing was the subject of hallucinations. The question was presented to a speaker about how to waken someone from a hallucination, which moved him to talk about what a hallucination was. He felt there was a possible connection between them and the REM sleep disorder that most LBD patients have. Something about the LBD brain blocks the normal paralysis that people experience when they sleep. Normal people are kept, for the most part, from acting out their dreams. Not so with LBD. The gate is wide open to their dreams, and they have a physical response to them. What if that open gate also allows the dream world to appear in their real physical world? These hallucinations that are "more real than real" to them could be their dream life entering into their consciousness. We all know how real some dreams seem to us, and that is why their hallucinations are so troubling to them.

The husband does not have that problem yet, thankfully.

He's A Scientist

March 11, 2019
Hayward, Wisconsin

I'm still coughing! Shortly after I came down with this cold that's making me miserable, the husband had something very similar, but of course, he doesn't have a cold. According to him, he is going through a phase of autophagy. He loves that word. It means clearing out the trash of damaged cells, and hopefully getting rid of some Lewy bodies. He thinks it's not a cold because his nasal drainage is clear, and because his magnesium supplement is working. I'm skeptical, as always. Looks like a cold to me.

Last night I went back through my emails and wrote down all the papers and research articles he's sent me over the last five or six weeks—27 in all, none of which I have read. I intend to read some, but I guess I'm reacting somewhat negatively to his obsessive behavior and preoccupation with his sickness. I get overwhelmed. Every conversation with him ends up connected to his health, his therapies, his symptoms. He is emphatic about supposed changes that he experiences, many of which are questionable. It goes beyond his own experience when he decides that everyone will benefit from his therapies by doing the same thing he is doing. He's a scientist, and he's excited.

I am toying with the idea of going to Seattle for a short visit, not that I want to travel, but because I want Esther (daughter) to know I care about her. Birthday week is coming up, and it's always hard to spend it alone with no fanfare.

I'm not sure I should leave Mom to deal with the husband by herself. She is sensitive to his plight and feels bad that she doesn't want to listen to all the things he wants to talk about. I'm not sure how to communicate to him that he would have to change in order for her to feel comfortable. I tried, but now I think he is feeling awkward. He feels that maybe Mom doesn't like him very much. I wish there were someone he could go live with for a few days while I'm gone.

He needs help all the time. Not for complicated things but for small stuff, like putting spaghetti in a dish and heating it up in the microwave. He gets brain fog and can't think what to do if the spaghetti noodles are cold and stuck together. It frustrates him.

I was asking him to cut his fingernails recently. When I see them so long that they look like a girl's fingernails, it really repels me, so I get the clippers out, ask him if he will do it, and then wait. I asked him if there was anything about the job that made it hard for him to want to do it regularly. He seemed genuinely happy to tell me that it was hard for him to see what he was doing. He couldn't press the clippers hard enough to get the job done. I clipped them for him. I also shaved him last week since he was having a hard time getting all the whiskers and would leave them in weird places, quite visible. Some of these things wouldn't be so hard if he kept with them on a regular basis, but he doesn't have a habit of doing that.

Yesterday, he was very emotional. He wanted me to know that he felt I was in a dangerous position if I were to decide to treat him like Job's wife (in the Bible) had treated Job. I wasn't too thrilled to hear that comparison. He did go on to explain that he was getting a lot more sympathy for what the woman must have been experiencing and that he could see the temptation for her to lose patience.

The wrap-up of this discussion had him sitting on the end of the bed, weeping, and telling me that he felt he had changed and wanted to make amends for the times that he had not been there for his family in the past. He wanted me to know and believe that he had changed. And I do believe his thinking has changed. It's a start, but behavior is largely determined by habit.

If author Dr. Carolyn Dean is correct about the magnesium deficiency that all of us are supposedly experiencing, I have a very long list of maladies I hope to see changing as I ingest more of it. Meanwhile, I will do what there is to do—exercise, try to eat well, keep good hours, keep happy, and avoid stress.

He Reads What I Write

March 27, 2019
Hayward, Wisconsin

As I've said before, this journey that the husband and I are on began years ago, way before I realized what it was.

Sometimes I ask, "Why him? Why me? Why us?" I've heard it said that we are what we think. I've heard it said that we are what we eat. I've heard it said that it's all up to genetics. I think it's a combination of all those things, some under our control and others not. I believe that God works with us in all of these things to create a life of a certain sort, unique to each person, and valuable to Him.

I'm thinking about all of this because, over the last half year, the things we have found out have been life-changing for us. I find that I'm living life with an awesome guy who now has this awful diagnosis. It's our journey together, but I need a place to share my thoughts, experiences, and observations without affecting him emotionally. I have been writing in my blog, but the husband, as I often refer to him, reads that. I put things there that I want him to know. He pays attention to things he reads, almost to the point of having a photographic memory. So I've decided to start a second blog for my more personal writing and the things that might upset him.

I'm not intending to be disrespectful in any way, but knowing my side of the story might, at times, be emotionally burdensome to him. He's a worrier. I'm not going to tell him about that blog. I'm naming it "Hope in the Face of Dementia" because being hopeful is one of his strong points.

In addition to working out my own thoughts, I want to encourage and connect with others who are having to get personal with the issue of dementia—Alzheimer's, LBD, or any others. It's not an easy journey, and it might help us to share our stories.

"Good company in a journey makes the way seem shorter,"[1] says Izaak Walton. I'm hoping he's right.

1 Walton, Izaak. *The Compleat Angler*. 1653. Edited by Arthur Waugh, Oxford UP, 1906.

Magnesium

March 29, 2019
Hayward, Wisconsin

Today we got our first shipment of Dr. Carolyn Dean's magnesium and mineral complex supplements. The husband has been very excited about starting them. It's the better form of magnesium that is absorbed immediately before leaving the stomach. It should not cause bowel irritation or diarrhea, so more of it can be taken. He is still sure he's very deficient and needs the maximum amount. He is sure that he's successfully untangling the amyloid protein bodies in his brain and restoring himself to normal.

He has been off his prescription meds for a little more than a week now. His blood pressure is sometimes high, but he is convinced it's his reaction to being upset at the time. He takes it again later, and it is a little lower, usually. In his view, magnesium has normalized his blood pressure.

He thinks his skin condition has improved, his other symptoms associated with his facial nerve have improved (eyesight and smell), and he feels he is moving more steadily. When we walk, he comments on how he can look around now, not at his feet constantly. And of course, he is not constipated. He has to tell that, even to strangers he has just met. He doesn't just tell them he's not constipated, no, it has to be the before and after story, with all kinds of details. It's weird.

Even though he sees improvement in his condition, there are still fluctuations to deal with. Things can change on an hourly basis, so it is hard to say the improvements are lasting. One thing I can say is that he doesn't seem to be getting worse. That is a hopeful thing for which I am thankful. Given a prognosis of 3-5 years, I'm feeling pretty positive about his present status. He's a scientist, so maybe he will find his way to a cure.

It's All Connected

March 30, 2019
Hayward, Wisconsin

I have a list of articles that the husband has been reading and discussing with his brother on the phone for the last couple of months. I don't think I will ever want to do all this reading, but I am certainly impressed with his zeal for learning.

His research often starts with a symptom he's experiencing and trying to understand. He uses Google on his phone and reads, then he forwards the link to his brother, who is a retired university biologist. One article will lead him to another one, and there is always a connection to be made to the next thing. Sometimes I can see his reasoning, and other times I think he's stretching things a bit.

A common thread is that he believes many of his symptoms have something to do with the magnesium deficiency he is sure he has. Magnesium is needed for so many functions on the cellular level that a deficiency could affect any organ system in the body. He believes correcting the deficiency could reverse the damage in the brain that causes diseases like Alzheimer's and Lewy body dementia. That's what he's trying to do—reverse things.

I can see the connection between his "research" and his often strange requests. The articles on magnesium and the book by Dr. Carolyn Dean would convince anyone they had a deficiency. So, I don't wonder about the PDF of magnesium-rich foods, or the articles connecting magnesium and red clay. But I do wonder how he stumbled on the subject of cheese and the sensation it gives him in his head when he eats it.

And there are his funny dance exercises that he does when his blood pressure is high, stemming from the article about nitric acid dumps. And the article about dietary buffers for cattle—what does that even mean? I'm afraid to ask. It sounds like something to do with electricity in dairy barns. I don't know where he's going with that.

The list is long, and I find it overwhelming. But it is so very typical of Dr. Dennis Dietz to tackle a problem in this manner, and I am glad to record that he is staying true to form. And he did it all scrolling on his phone, making the print as large as it would go. Quite a feat.

Faithfulness

April 3, 2019
Hayward, Wisconsin

Last week we went to church and sang "Great Is Thy Faithfulness." As he began to talk to us, the pastor wanted three people to tell of God's faithfulness in their lives. I always jump up at this kind of invitation. It's not that I have it in mind to say a particular thing, but I know God has been faithful and I should say so.

I stumbled around a bit, explaining the difficulty of moving to a new area and then getting word that my husband has dementia. It has had its depressing moments, circumstances that we weren't happy about, but we go through each day able to find the goodness of God toward us. I said something to that effect.

As I finished, the husband raised his hand and said, in his raspy Lewy voice, "And I wouldn't have it any other way".

I know what he meant by that. We have talked about it numerous times. He has felt an actual friendship with Jesus and had dreams (I think he would call them that) where he's been given words to think about and investigate. Jesus knows he's a scientist and loves to figure things out, so He gives the husband clues that lead to more clues. If he gets stuck and doesn't know what comes next, he asks and waits until Jesus tells him more. He's very touched by this friendship and gets emotional relating the details.

It's never been his choice to have this diagnosis, of course, but knowing that God has allowed it for a reason, he is accepting it. The resulting relationship with God and with friends and relatives has enriched the experience beyond what he would have expected in life. In that sense, he wouldn't have wanted it any other way, because the good probably wouldn't have come any other way. God knows how to arrange what we need to have happen.

Interruptions

April 4, 2019
Hayward, Wisconsin

This morning, back at home, I am writing with frequent interruptions. As I tried to watch the sunrise and have my morning coffee at 6:30, the husband also got up and came out wanting to talk about ordinary things.

"What is the temperature?"

"The sun is in my eyes, can you lower the shade?"

"I only had to get up once last night."

"I've learned to control my drooling by lightly pressing on C-3."

"Do we have earbuds so I can talk to my brother without using a speakerphone?"

Mom has explained to me that she isn't trying to be mean by going to her room and shutting the door all the time. She just can't take the constant interruptions and engagement on the subjects of the husband's choice. It even bothers her to hear his telephone calls, which he makes for hours at a time. But she says she is ok living in her bedroom, and I notice she now has a dining table with salt, pepper, and her own small coffee maker in there. I miss her and the times we would spend talking in the morning.

It's often the choice now between meeting my own needs for fellowship and leaving the husband rather obviously segregated, or staying out with him to meet his need for some kind of socialization. Why is he getting up so early now? Was it depression that kept him sleeping until 10 every morning before? And now he's all excited and hopeful?

We can't figure it out. We'll have to take it one day at a time. Things are always changing.

Trying to Sleep

April 30, 2019
Hayward, Wisconsin

Bedtime is often early—7 or 8 pm, after an early dinner. Around 9, just when I think I will have some undisturbed time to read or write, I will hear him get out of bed and shuffle to the door and peer around the corner at me while I sit at my desk. He will do a silly little wave and announce his first wake-up of the night.

Tonight, he came out and sat down next to me as I wrote. He waited until I looked at him and then told me that he wanted to talk to me. Conversations that start like this are often ones I don't like.

What he wanted was for me to document the phase that he was in. It's a problem that happens at night, and this is how he describes it. It's tension that keeps him awake, a bit like restless leg syndrome. He feels that his blood pressure is high and that he needs to have more magnesium water. He wants very much to sit and somehow resolve this tension, but knows that he must do something active instead.

I suggested he take his blood pressure to see if it was high, but the act of getting up and putting the cuff on to take the reading was something he felt would cause more tension. He didn't want to do it, but finally relented, only if I would go get the cuff and put it on him. Paradoxically, the next thing he needed to do was what he calls his "high intensity exercise moves." He admitted the contradiction.

His blood pressure reading was 167/95 with a pulse of 49. He got up to do his exercises, which were mostly arm movements and a little bit of squatting. He insisted that it be recorded that his hands began to tingle, and he felt the stimulation up the back of his neck, and of course, he got tired and breathed a little heavier. He explained that all this was important to note because it showed that he didn't have to do a lot of exercise to get what he called a nitric acid dump. This was an exercise protocol he learned from some online coach. After exercise, his blood pressure was higher—183/106, pulse 58, which he predicted would happen. He rested for a while and drank more magnesium water until his pressure was back down to the pre-exercise level. I listened calmly to all of this and made an effort to look understanding.

From his reading, he has a mental construct of what he thinks is going on in his body. Although I am a nurse and remember a lot of anatomy and physiology, much of what he says sounds mysterious to me. Taking his blood pressure puts pressure on his bladder? His body starts clearing out bad cells a certain number of hours after he eats and makes him have to clear his throat and spit? Makes him have to urinate, and makes him need more and more magnesium? But okay, maybe, I think. I keep listening.

Something makes him feel that the whole process is speeding up and requiring more magnesium. He used to sip on one 16 oz. bottle of water with 300 mg magnesium per day and possibly another one during the night. Now he is asking for at least two and sometimes three. He asks me to help him mix this concoction, because measuring the minerals is difficult for him. He shakes and spills some of the magnesium, and it is precious stuff.

He believes the nighttime spitting and urinating are clearing the misfolded proteins out of his brain. He feels like a scientist, taking part in a groundbreaking experiment, which must be recorded.

I don't know how to adequately portray the drama involved as he tells me these things. To him, it's life-changing stuff. He wants me to record it for future reference. I can do that, I assured him. And then, I helped him get back to bed.

PART THREE:
THE LBD ROLLER COASTER

What He Thinks

May 25, 2019
Hayward, Wisconsin

What will today bring? That is what I think to myself each day as I wake and take stock of the time, and where the husband is. Today, he was asleep initially, got up once to visit the bathroom, and then went back to bed until nearly 10 am. Even Mom was wondering about him and asked me how he was—was he alive?

As I watched him get out of bed, he told me he wanted to see David Kelling, the chiropractor. He was pretty sure that what he had eaten the night before was not good for him. He had decided that the meatballs must have had pork in them, and he wanted to find out if David knew how long it would take for him to purge himself of the effect. The effect was mostly his fatigue, and sleeping longer than usual. "Clean" and "unclean" foods have increased relevance to him since watching one of the TBN preachers on the subject.

He decided that fasting was the order of the day for him, but he did want to pray with me for the meal I was having for breakfast. He remarked about how different it was for him to be praying for my breakfast, while praying for his fast, asking that they would both be good. For several minutes I was able to distract him with news of people we had known in Florida, but soon we were back on the subject of health, only it was now my health.

According to his observation, I thrash around in my sleep a lot, and he is unable to wake me lately to get me to stop. Behind this topic is his supposition that I have REM sleep disorder, which means I'm just like him, only a few years behind in progression. My symptoms should move me to take more magnesium, quickly.

He was able to sit and lift one leg up onto the opposite knee without using his hands to pull it up. He has been doing this the last couple of days, meaning that he is improving his strength and flexibility. Everything he does better than the day before is because his therapies are working. Everything he does worse is because of something he did wrong—the wrong supplement, the wrong food, not enough exercise... The fluctuations are never because of LBD and its usual course. Sometimes he looks sad, and he may be thinking of the LBD, but he does not acknowledge it.

I looked at his blood pressure log yesterday and noticed that he hasn't recorded anything for almost two weeks. This was an obsession not too long ago, needing to be done every time he "felt" any change. I don't know if he's forgotten or if he believes his pressure is normal now and no longer needs to be monitored, since he stopped taking all his medications. Yes, he did that. Dr. Chambers told him it wasn't the smartest thing to do since he still had some high readings, and having a stroke would put an end to all his other therapies. He didn't agree. He is getting better.

In spite of getting better, he has come out for help putting on his shirt and just came out to tell me what a terrible time he had putting a different belt through his belt loops while trying to keep his shorts on.

He has taken to heart what he heard from another preacher on TV, about being selfless and thinking of others. Twice this week, he has insisted upon riding in the back seat of the car and letting Mom have the front. He makes sure it gets talked about and noticed. He's trying.

I Get a Vacation

May 25, 2019
Hayward, WI

I took a vacation. It was an epic hike to the bottom of the Grand Canyon, tenting there for three nights, and hiking back up. It was planned last year, involving expense and arrangements with other people so I could not easily change the plan, although I considered doing that. To be gone for seven days required more effort and stress for others than I had thought it would.

I am glad that I had the foresight to ask our youngest daughter, Esther, if she could come to stay while I was gone. She was able to keep her father company and to help her grandmother not feel the whole weight of his socialization. I also wanted feedback on my own observations and assessments. I don't always know if I am seeing what I think I'm seeing, or if I'm just being impatient and somewhat biased because of my closeness to the issue.

There were hard moments for both of them—Esther confirmed this—but overall she did a great job of making him happy and helping him feel guided and informed. She gave him tips on calming himself, on exercising with dance, and being lighthearted and silly as therapy. They talked. They did things together. It was good for him and good for their relationship. I am grateful for all she supplied, but also aware of the cost for her. Taking solo vacations is probably not something I will be doing a lot.

However, we can take vacations together, the husband and I. And that will be another adventure, I'm sure.

Endless Discussion

May 27, 2019
Hayward, WI

Yesterday, because I was visibly sad, the husband and I had several conversations about our relationship. I tried to tell him, without being harsh, why it is that I have trouble taking him seriously or relying on his decisions and assessments. I know it must be hard to hear that kind of thing. I don't think he understood, and he still thinks that I am wrong in taking his LBD diagnosis into consideration. He thinks everything points toward his recovery.

We had discussions about the carbon monoxide alarm that went off at 4 am, which he is sure is because of variations in the power grid. We should call the power company and have them do something about it. He doesn't say what.

We had discussions about tithing the proceeds from the sale of the house, about how to identify where the Lord wants tithe administered, and about who can decide these things.

We had a discussion about the supplements he ordered and wants to return, thinking he doesn't need them now because he is no longer on blood pressure meds. There is no trace of where to get that money ($250) back that I am aware of, and he is useless in tracking things on his phone or computer.

He went to church twice yesterday to hear piano player Huntley

Brown. He sang his heart out and greatly enjoyed the music and worship, but was totally worn out by the effort. He got tired in the morning just making one side of the bed. Somehow, the tiredness became my fault for helping him with chores. According to him, our invalid Aunt Lois is also tired all the time because I help her too much, keeping her from getting stronger.

In many respects, he is like a child in an old man's body. I can tell when he is coming by his slow, shuffling sound. He always appears very old and slow. He does unusual things, like standing up in church and directing the music, waving his arms, but he is innocent and entirely abandoned in his actions. He feels no shame and is joyful and unaware of strangeness. He doesn't care what others think or how they perceive him, and that is the child part. I don't want to take that from him, but it puts me in the position of being a caregiver for someone who is not quite "with it" rather than a partner in an equal relationship. I have to be the one who considers all sides of an issue and whether to affirm or deny his course of action.

In all our discussions, I primarily wanted to be understood, but I don't see that it happened. To his credit, he was always sincere and soft spoken, which was helpful. I took a walk late in the evening and encountered my brother and sister-in-law, who joined me. They listened to me, and I was comforted just to know that someone cared about my tears and would let me talk.

I struggle right now with a sense of displacement. Our house in Florida has finally sold. We are to leave Mom's condo and set ourselves up in a neighboring one. We need to decide whether to get our stuff in North Carolina transferred up here. We need to start paying rent.

Everything about our situation seems to have changed, and I'm trying to sort it all out. I need God to reassure me that we are here for a reason and that we are still in His will and plan for us. I have attitudes and feelings that I'm not comfortable with, but I don't know how to dispel them.

New Day, New Problem

June 3, 2019
Hayward, WI

I have to write about this because I am so conflicted. Is this really as crazy as it sounds, or is there some validity to what my husband is thinking and experiencing? I know he really is experiencing something—but is it LBD, or what a normal person would experience if they were extra sensitive? It's all about electricity.

This week, to my surprise, a big Excel Energy truck came to our driveway. The husband had called in a complaint about low voltage. He has been developing his theory about why our smoke alarm and CO alarm have been sounding at 4 am. He has added, as proof that something is wrong, any instance of alarms going off in any building in our development. I don't know how he finds out about things happening in other people's houses.

When we started having trouble with the TV he watched in Mom's condo, that also became part of the low voltage problem. Now, he is sure the TV in our new condo has problems because of low voltage.

The other night, he came back from dinner at a restaurant and was abnormally tired the minute he stepped in the house. He decided it was electromagnetic waves, energy gone rogue in the house, that were dangerous. He didn't want to sleep in the house. He didn't want me to sleep in the house either. Later, he was panicking and woke me up to tell me how scared he was. To him, the fact that he had to call me more than once to wake me was evidence that I was already affected. I couldn't think of anything to do to calm him, except pray with him.

He did finally sleep, but remained convinced he was being harmed. His nerves are super sensitive, and he knew something was wrong. Amazingly, we lived through the night.

In the morning, he didn't say much, but he wanted to stay out of buildings, both our condo and my mother's, away from the energy fields that weakened him.

That morning, as I worked in the garden, he called me, all excited. He had figured out the problem. After drinking some milk and eating some peanut butter, his thinking had cleared (peanut butter does that), and he remembered eating Cajun potatoes at the restaurant the night before. He was sure they had enzymes in the spices that had weakened him. Of course. To him, it made perfect sense.

Rogue Voltage

June 4, 2019
Hayward, WI

He's just going to live outside from now on...

Two more days have passed since the husband had his first major panic about the electrical energy in our house. Things have not gotten better since. He has honed his theory that the natural voltage between the sky and the earth is affecting him bodily. He feels it the minute he steps into the house. He has caught the idea of "earthing" and grounding himself to the earth, which he knows is going to help him feel so much better. To me, it sounds like an ad he's seen on Facebook.

The day before last, he sat outside, where he felt safe, fell asleep, and got a horrible sunburn on one side of his face. It blistered and was weepy, then crusty. He doesn't want to sleep in the house at night unless we turn off all the electricity. I admit, I flipped the main breaker for the sake of getting some peace. He keeps saying that if he has a good night, it will prove that it is the electrical fault in the house causing the problem. There could be no other reason for a good night's sleep.

He is pretty much in denial about his LBD, and I can't blame him. He doesn't quite accept that, apart from a healing miracle, he is probably dying of dementia. It happens. He still tells people he is getting better and will once again do the things he has done, like playing his trumpet.

He rode along with Mom and me to Duluth today for an appointment with Mom's dermatologist. With his sunburned, damaged face, he looked like he was the patient needing help. On the way home, he was looking out the window at the sky and saw a strange cloud formation. To him, it looked man-made. It was quite diffuse and included jet trails, wide and fading, that fanned out like the spokes of a wagon wheel. Later at home, he heard there was a bad storm near Duluth. Right away, he attributed it to the government experimenting with weather control—the chemtrails and clouds proved it. They were too unusual to be anything else. He has so many new fears now that keep him on the lookout.

He spent the rest of the night looking up articles and people who would attest to what he thinks is true. Some of the articles are on earthing—walking around with bare feet in contact with the ground. From there, he went to order a special blanket that acts like a Faraday cage, which will protect him from voltage. Every time he stands up, he says, "Okay, I'm about to get full voltage again, and I don't know what I'm going to do." He says he can't live like this (and I agree, totally, for different reasons).

He talked about renting a different condo, but I can't see that another building would be any different from the one we are in, which was built to code recently. I told him I wasn't moving. I'm not sure what he decided, but he has come up with something that has enabled him to go to sleep in the bedroom. I don't think he has noticed that I turned the electricity back on.

All this has changed his focus. Lately, he has not been fixated on his supplements, and he doesn't eat as much as usual either—big changes for him.

A Hard Thing

June 6, 2019
Hayward, WI

This hard thing happens every time the husband comes up with a new thought about his theory of the day. He looks at me dramatically with a horrified expression on his face and explains the newest evidence of the connection between electricity and the way he is feeling.

Today, his thoughts have been directed to the ants who have nests in the ground around our house, small red ants that are common everywhere. He tells me that it is a well-known fact that they are drawn to electrical current, citing several experiences with ant nests in electrical boxes and outlets. He has gone around outside the house, locating any pile of sand that the ants have deposited and lining it up with an electrical outlet inside the house. When asked what that means for us and what we should do about it, he says that we should get the house properly grounded. I remind him that it is already grounded to code and more (yesterday's episode), and he then remarks about the age of the water heater, as if that cancels out the electrical grounding.

Last week, he insisted on buying a grounding mat for the bed. I spent several hours researching the ones he was looking at and finally did the ordering for him. I decided it would be worth the expense if it would buy him some peace of mind. I even bought a smaller grounding mat for his feet when sitting in his chair.

The first night, the effect was too much, although I'm not sure how one gets too grounded. We tried putting a sheet between him and the mat. When that didn't feel right either, he decided two sheets would be better. When that didn't feel right, he presumed the sheets weren't effective because they were polyester. When he found out they were both 100% cotton, he had no answer, but he still couldn't sleep on the mat. Please send it back.

Taking It All In

June 12, 2019
Hayward, WI

There have been several poignant moments today. In one of them, I could tell that my loved one, "LO" as they say in the support group, was feeling very emotional.

He was standing listening to a song, "It Is Well with My Soul," and was clearly losing his composure—this, in front of our good friends visiting from Florida. I hugged him and helped him sway to the music. We danced, or something close to that, for the remainder of the song. He was able to quiet himself and come to the breakfast table with us. I can only imagine how frightening his life is now.

Later, we were meeting with our pastor over a matter of great concern to us both. I had promised him he could talk and tell the pastor whatever he wanted to tell him. They talked for 90 minutes. One of the things that came out was his recollection of me saying that he was not the man I thought he was when I married him. He wanted to admit that he had not been fully present in some of his family duties. His evidence that I felt that way was that I referred to him in my writing as "the husband," not by his name, Dennis. This was the first time I had heard this, and I was a little shocked to learn how he felt about it. It is easily remedied, and I will try to call him Dennis more often.

The last thing on today's list of new realities was hearing Dennis's announcement of finding new articles proving the connection between electrical sensitivity and Lewy body dementia. Once again, he is alarmed anew, to the extent of experiencing chest pain. Our proximity to power lines is an imminent danger to him, to me, and to all our family. Nothing anyone has said about this matter has changed his narrative. He returns to it again and again. I'm wondering if this is what the support group refers to as looping.

I also read something alarming today. There is a statistic that says 40% of caregivers die before their patient does, for various reasons (neglect of their own health, stress, etc.). Although I aim to be among the 60% who don't, I have to admit that it is stressful to repeatedly hear about how I am in grave danger. I am on the road to self-destruction if I don't heed the warnings of my husband, Dennis.

Our World Gets Smaller

June 15, 2019
Hayward, WI

This is so frightening.

Dennis came out of the bedroom this morning and every sentence out of his mouth was full of anxiety and on the edge of panic.

"You need to be taking this, too (magnesium), and the proteolytic enzymes as well."

"You need to be watching your protein intake and getting enough."

"You need to take your tea and go sit by the grounding mat. You need to get grounded right away."

"You need to spend as much time as possible away from the house, outside."

"If you want to talk with me, come into the bedroom and sit on the bed (with its grounding mat)."

"We are one. You have the same thing I do. I saw you getting sleepy last night. You could hardly keep your eyes open."

He goes into the bedroom like he says he will, but reappears every minute or so with another directive. Even though he says he has figured out that his distress the other night was from the Cajun spices (in his Greek chicken wrap...). He says the electrical issue is not solved. We must resolve it. I will probably be hearing how that is to be done all day.

Is there hope of this going away?

Father's Day

June 16, 2019
Hayward, WI

Today was Father's Day. It was not a bad day, but in some ways a sad day.

The best part was that we left the house early for church, ate breakfast afterwards at a restaurant, and then stayed outside away from electric fields all day. At least that was the way I saw it.

Dennis talked to both his daughters on the phone today, and listening to those conversations was the sad part. He has changed so much, even in the last two weeks—rambling, sometimes confused, distracted by clouds in the sky or his own thoughts. In his account of the day, he mentioned a major mistake he (we) made. I didn't agree, but it made no difference.

I decided that since we had such a nice rest in the truck the day before, why not just drive our truck out in the wetland meadow behind the barn and he could spend as much time there as he wanted. Why not, indeed? So, we did that. I found a nice shade tree to park under, repositioned the truck several times, rehearsed with him how to open or shut windows, and then I left. He could call me on his phone if he needed anything—I would be only a short distance away.

He stayed there several hours while I did some work, and he only called me twice. I went out to check on him, and he was so busy talking on the phone that I left again and went to the house to do chores.

His next call to me was about his mistake. He hadn't been thinking and had wasted a few hours already by not being grounded. The truck, because it had rubber tires, was not grounded unless a chain or something metal was touching the earth. He was having to get out of the truck and put his feet down and walk around to remedy the situation. He wanted to know if I could bring the walker out so he could sit on the seat and still have his feet on the ground. Yes, I could. I even brought him a snack and his magnesium water. After all, it was Father's Day.

I heard him repeat the story twice to our daughters later. After hearing it the first time, I asked him why he needed to be grounded if there were no electric fields, no EMFs in sight, but he didn't answer—just shook his head. I guess I don't really understand electricity (along with a lot of other things...).

Exactly What?

June 17, 2019
Hayward, WI

What exactly am I to do?

He came shuffling from the bedroom where he had gone to sleep and found me, still working on the computer. I dread the sound of him coming because I know he is going to tell me some new reason why he has to get out of this house.

"Do you see this?" He held up his hand with the fingers curled nearly shut. "My hand was frozen like this. Locked. I couldn't move it." His face had that look. Haunted, bleary-eyed, almost motionless even when talking and trying to be dramatic.

I didn't know what to say. "You have a movement disorder, a Parkinsonian problem that is common with Lewy body. How do you want to remedy the situation?"

"There is no remedy here. I have to get out of this place." He teetered and caught himself as he turned and shuffled out again.

I thought for a while and followed him into the dark bedroom. We talked. I was desperate. He was desperate. In frustration, I told him to get his clothes on and get in the truck. I'd take him somewhere remote and we would both sleep there tonight. He refused my offer. The truck is not grounded, so it wouldn't do any good.

He's so good at throwing something crazy back at me, almost like a test, but he doesn't think it's crazy at all. He wants to call Mayo Clinic and see what they do for this. They're here in the Midwest, where there are lots of dairy farms with grounding problems. (What?! And then I remember one of his research articles.) They probably have people with this same thing and know what to do.

To call sounds ridiculous to me, and I'm pretty sure I know what Mayo Clinic will think when they see his diagnosis, but it is something I can do. I can ask. Will that satisfy him? I tell him they aren't going to get back to him tonight.

He knows that. "They'll probably just tell me to get away from the house." Yeah, probably.

Camping Out

June 18, 2019
Hayward, WI

I was in such a cooperative mood today—determined to help this guy feel comfortable somewhere other than in the house. I told him we were going to set up a camp out in the field. We could go out in the truck and put up a tent. How could that not work? But here were the problems:

Tent has a polyethylene floor so it's not grounded

Nothing to plug the grounding pad into

Truck would not be grounded either—yesterday's mistake

Must find ohmmeter so we can tell if we're conducting anything

Must have multiple things to sit on, besides truck, for comfort

Must have peanut butter, cheese, and magnesium water

Must be in the shade in case it's hot

Must have jacket

Must have head pillow

On and on...

We spent quite a while fixing alligator clamps from the ohmmeter onto a grounding spike, which was really a huge metal file I had scrounged from the workbench. This contraption was then attached to the truck to ground it. He figured he could ground himself by holding on to another wire attached to the same spike. When we got out to the field and set up the chair, the snacks, the ground wires, and the grounding pad on the chair, I was all set for a good time tending the garden while he communed with nature and his phone.

Less than an hour later, I was getting phone calls from him. The grounding wasn't working and he knew why. Next came the call saying that he and the walker had made it back to the house and couldn't get in because the back door was locked (um... try the front door, it's not).

Next, where is the remote that changes the channels on the TV?

Next, bathroom problems.

I gave up and went to the house. Later, I walked back to the truck, loaded everything up and drove it all back. So much for camping out. Not doing that again.

Fluctuations

June 19, 2019
Hayward, WI

I am so glad there has been a gradual change over the last couple of days. I don't know if it has been because I asked him to quit taking proteolytic enzymes for a few days, or perhaps it's just a Lewy fluctuation. Either way, I'll take it and be thankful because this has been a stressful week and a half.

Last night, there was no begging to go elsewhere to sleep. He slept part of the time in bed and part of the time in the recliner. He came and got me every time he needed to change something, and that was a bit reminiscent of my night shifts as a private duty nurse, but overall, we were peaceful.

He did want to get out of the house early this morning and go to breakfast at the Family Restaurant. That was good news because I'll take breakfast out most any time. He figured getting away would help him recover from the hours spent overnight in the electric field. He wanted to sound intelligent at our meeting with the financial advisor at 10.

Breakfast was over by 8 am, so he wanted to hang out at the church—just on a whim. It was open. (Are churches always open anymore? I don't know.) Dennis went in and actually fell asleep in a comfy chair in the Fireside Room. I spent some peaceful time alone in the sanctuary playing the piano. It was a good choice, and I'm keeping it in mind for the future.

Even while we were doing these other things, Dennis had something else in the back of his mind. He had asked me to contact an electrician again. Even though I had called twice, the man was not calling back, not even to say he was too busy to check out our "grounding problem." Dennis had figured out a new angle during the night, and at breakfast, he had made me write down the specific points he wanted the electrician to check on. So the electrical craziness had not gone away by any means.

Fortunately, later in the morning, one of his phone contacts, whom he greatly admires, told him he was thinking wrongly about electricity. He actually started to consider if that could be true. The result was that he didn't have to be on any grounding pads all day, he quit wearing his "grounding moccasins" with the lining cut out, and he actually thinks it is good now to be insulated FROM the ground. Go figure...

Tonight he was able to talk coherently, see almost normally, check his own email on his phone, get himself out of chairs and the sofa without difficulty, and was CHEERFUL. Wow. He ate supper and has decided to sleep on the futon in the sunroom, which is fine. Maybe I'll get some sleep tonight.

A Spiritual Experience

June 20, 2019
Hayward, WI

If it were not for hugs, sometimes I would not know what to do to preserve the relationship between my husband and myself. Sometimes it is all we can do. We have to quit talking and hug. We often hit an impasse when he attributes his symptoms to something other than Lewy body and I remind him that LBD is the most likely cause of most of his symptoms. "That's just a name. Nobody really knows what it is or what causes it," he will tell me. Also, he is onto something big that may prevent LBD and other dementias. It's something that God wants him to pursue, record, and publish.

He wavers. Every now and then, he wonders if he has heard correctly what God is saying to him. He will even think that LBD is something God is using to get his attention and correct him in his ways. He will get very introspective and cry. He even concludes that God could want him to quit trying to convince others and trust instead. But he cannot quit thinking, researching, and striving. The next time fear or anxiety strikes, he is right back in the game. There is always a new plan to present to me first, then to whomever he can get to listen and perhaps act.

One morning after requesting a serious talk, he told me that he would never hold it against me or others for not understanding. It was his fault for not being able to explain it well enough. I told him it was not a matter of understanding, it was a matter of believing. To him, his theories are facts that others should be able to understand. To others, his theories are just that, theories. And they are not the most likely explanation for what is happening to him.

He often suspects that I have been leading people to view him as unreliable in his ability to think and reason. He requests that I not do this, and he especially wants me to "change my song" when talking to him. He gets frustrated with me but is not angry, just very persistent. For that, I am thankful.

He is seeing his illness as a very spiritual experience. He hears God speaking through it, and I agree that some of the things he hears are right on target. He has changed his mind on some important issues. But after he feels he has gotten the lesson and accepted God's correction, he then looks for physical healing and wonders why God is withholding it. Then doubt, guilt, depression, and self-pity come rushing back in.

He is more in touch with his feelings than ever before in his life. He cries nearly every day. He is not crazy. He talks knowledgeably about many things. But some of his conclusions and his obsessions make people question him, and they would do that even if I told them nothing.

Higher Ground Please

June 22, 2019
Hayward, WI

The last few days, we have been several places away from home, seeking relief from the electric fields. We have spoken with electricians, we have prayed and battled spiritually, we have actually changed course and are no longer using grounding pads anywhere.

Dennis has had some new symptoms, and I'm sure they alarm him. For one, he has trouble swallowing his many pills. They are all supplements, so it's not critical that he take them if he has trouble. This symptom was addressed at the conference we went to, so it is an alarming occurrence for him.

Another surprise was when he mentioned hallucinations. He thought he saw me coming toward him out in the field today, but I wasn't. He thought he saw a man outside the window, but whenever he turned to see who it was, the man was gone. He said the "H word" himself.

But mostly it is still the electricity issue that is on his mind—trying to figure out why he feels tingling in his hands, cold extremities, dry mouth but drooling at the same time (???), and changes in his mental and emotional status whenever he is on our property and especially in our condo.

He would explain it this way. The code is written for single residences, but ours is a duplex. He looked up the code and found that it was a minimal requirement and didn't take safety fully into account. The building is grounded by two 10-foot rods. He feels that electricity from one grounding rod is conducted through the grounding rod into the wet ground (high water table) and feeds back into the other grounding rod and into our house through the neutral electric wire. Somehow, this translates into the theory that if he gets up high enough above the water table, his symptoms will lessen, perhaps go away. The rogue electric current is denaturing the protein in his body and creating more Lewy bodies faster than he can get rid of them with his magnesium water.

He talks about these theories/facts endlessly, and I finally am telling him to leave me out of the conversation. I am not going to help him research electromagnetic shielding on the internet. I don't want to hear about the dairy farms where this happens commonly, according to him. I am not going to try to lower the water table (he has ideas on how) or dig up the grounding rods and pull them out of the water.

As he says, he is sorry to be so much trouble, but the house, and really the whole residential development, is killing him and he has to get out.

I have never seen desperation like this.

The Non-Electric Meadow

June 24, 2019
Hayward, the meadow

Last night I thought we did rather well. Dennis slept in one bed all night. He got up to the bathroom several times, but seemed to be sleeping quietly the rest of the time. I hadn't flipped the main breaker, so the electricity was on too, and he didn't talk much about feeling symptoms.

Nevertheless, this morning he asked how soon we could leave the house. I had agreed that we would ask a friend in Duluth if we could stay with them for a couple of nights—just to see if being in their house, high on a hill, would satisfy the electrical sensitivity problem that "we" were having. They had extended the invitation, but I was considering the difficulty of getting Dennis up their long staircase to the one and only bathroom on the second floor.

Talking this over with Mom after church, she suddenly came up with an idea. "Why don't you try going out to the meadow first? It's close, it's high ground, and there's no electricity at all."

The meadow is a property about six miles from town, owned by Mom as part of the family estate. It was part of the farm that I grew up on. It was always a favorite place for my brothers, especially the eldest of them, to hunt and just be out in nature. It's actually 80 acres that's about half field and half forest. Just inside the forested part is a large clearing that brother Ron has been tending. He has planted it with good grass, cleared trails in the surrounding woods, and spends time improving it when he's up on vacation. Along one border, tucked in close to the trees, is an old house trailer, put there by my Dad, that the family uses on the rare occasions when staying out there overnight. I don't know why I didn't think of it before when searching for an unelectrified place. Probably because I didn't really want to leave home at all.

So, I packed up some things, and we went to check it out. Other than getting there and finding it was locked, we've had no real problems. We had to go back for the key, and I went back again for a few things that I forgot, but all told, the husband has been here for five hours now and is happy. He's either been sleeping or eating, both of which have been hard for him when affected by the electric field at home. He claims to feel wonderful, although he still has symptoms, which he attributes to all the damage that has been happening for the last few weeks.

I am very interested in seeing how this first night out here goes for him. No electricity, no water except what we bring in jugs, no working bathroom, and smelling like mice—but way better than any tent, for sure. It's easy for him to get into, has a bed he likes, chairs, a table, and a couch. What more could a man want? Will this give him the opportunity to recover from LBD like he thinks it will? Will this give him time to write his book? He thinks so, and this is why he's so happy.

The meadow is beautiful with waist-high grasses. A moment ago, I saw a deer strolling through, grazing as it went. It's peaceful here. I just have to figure out how to fit this into the rest of life, if it's the only way Dennis can feel good. Unlike him, I have other responsibilities, but at least I've been able to honor his request to "get me out of here!" I have to do this just in case there's a chance that it truly is an electric field that has caused him to deteriorate so rapidly.

Night Two at the Meadow

June 26, 2019
Hayward, the meadow

He woke two times during the night, and the chief complaint was that he was cold. In spite of sleeping in his stocking hat, down shirt, hoodie, socks, and pajama pants, he was not getting warm under the comforter. It was a queen-size bed and he had it all to himself. I was on the couch, in a sleeping bag with an annoying zipper that got stuck every time I had to get out to help him.

I don't know what the temp was inside our trailer, but the weather app said it was 59 degrees outside. His first remark, besides how cold he was, was about the sky temperature and one of his friends being right about radiant heat, blah, blah, blah... I had to laugh (inwardly) at his observation during the night when I was up helping him, standing around in my T-shirt and underwear. "I'm glad you have more fat than I do, to keep you warm," he said. He followed up with a disclaimer that he didn't mean I was fat, just that I had more fat than he did. I know he feels he has lost weight (can't keep his pants up), but even with that, the remark was funny.

My plan to warm him up was to get the truck going, stick him in it, and go to breakfast in some nice warm place with coffee. And so, we were at the Robin's Nest Cafe at 7 when it opened.

Sometime in the last few weeks, he has lost sight of the reasons he used to have for eating keto. Protein has become a naughty word now, because the Lewy bodies are misfolded proteins. It's now complex carbohydrates all the way. He had a big breakfast of oatmeal, raisin toast, and one egg. That's why I was surprised, after a couple of hours hanging out at the church, that he was hungry again and wanted to ask Mom to go to lunch with us. We picked her up at 1 pm and went to Norske Nook, and again were stuffed.

In going over to pick Mom up, I discovered that he now doesn't even want to be in the driveways of either of our condos. Five minutes in the car, in the driveway, sets his progress back. He can feel the electricity. I parked a distance away near the garden, where he thought it would be okay, but he told me when I came back that it wasn't a good spot either.

Is this really our life for the future? In order to have any time in my own home I have to take him back to the meadow and leave him there. That's what I did. He insisted that I bring my brother's propane heater out, in case it got cold again tonight. And tied up in all this is the sky temperature, which is evidently much colder than it should be because "they" are seeding it. Climate manipulation.

His most prevalent problem is with delusion and the "foggy" forgetful times. The delusion is persistent. The forgetfulness comes and goes minute by minute and always surprises me. Today, he forgot how to get to the bathroom in the church, a place he has been dozens of times. He doesn't hear because he won't wear his hearing aids, and he sees more poorly all the time and comments about it. He is disabled to the point that it is a big deal for him to be able to put on his shirt, pick something up from the floor, or get out of bed by himself.

I don't recognize our life anymore.

What Bothers Me Most

June 26, 2019
Hayward, the meadow

What bothers me—well, it all bothers me because it is so sad and not what either of us wanted for our "golden years." But what bothers me to the point that I feel it in my gut, and play it over and over in my mind, is when he starts diagnosing me and wanting me to follow his advice.

Early on, in the magnesium stage, he would tell me that I was flapping my arms in my sleep and breathing funny. I needed to be on magnesium right away.

If I forget anything, even for a moment, dementia is setting in, and I get a knowing look.

In the middle of the night, I have found him standing by my side of the bed, insisting that I drink some water because he had a hard time waking me. I was dehydrating to death, I guess.

If I get sleepy during the day, it's the electric field dulling my mind, pushing me into unconsciousness.

Last night, he was frightened by how long I supposedly went without breathing and insisted that I get a cap to cover my head from the cold—the obvious solution. Nights are the craziest.

I tried to reason with him this morning, and in the process, he pointed out that, intellectually, I had to admit that, when sleeping, how could I possibly be aware of what I was doing? I pointed out to him that someone who has bad hearing, limited eyesight, and tends to be fearful is probably not capable of making assessments in the middle of the night either, intellectually. It made no difference. I have to learn to listen and reassure, then dismiss so it doesn't vex me for hours after.

VEX, a word that even looks like it feels.

Two Lives

June 28, 2019
Hayward, WI

Tonight we fell asleep with the scent of newly mown hay. The meadow and the larger field by the road were mowed today by a nearby farmer who rents the field. The waist-high grass and clover are down, and hopefully there will be a dry day tomorrow to prepare for baling.

I have two separate and very different lives.

In one of them, I am single and living in a nice condo with my cat, Shadow. I live next to my mom and close to my brother and sister-in-law. I work in the garden pulling weeds and planting vegetables. I walk the surrounding wetlands and take pictures of geese. I work twice a week at my brother's business, where I edit and sometimes write in his business blog and clean and empty trash. I grocery shop, wash clothes, and all those ordinary things.

Today, in my single life, I lay out a jigsaw puzzle, turning all 1,000 pieces right side up and putting together the edges. I watered the petunias and talked with my mom.

In my other life, I am married to Dennis (the husband), and I live in Smith Meadow in a travel trailer. I light candles and use flashlights to see at night since there is no electricity. I carry water from town in plastic jugs since there is no well. There isn't an outhouse either, so it's a good thing I know how to dig holes and bury. I have a propane heater borrowed from my brother that I can fire up if it gets too cold at night. And (very importantly) I have another small camp stove to heat water for my morning coffee.

Our perishable food is in a cooler, and I replenish the ice almost daily. I take a couple trips into town every day. I shop for things we need. I bring my husband liver and onions from the local restaurant. He isn't well, and this place is where he feels safe for the time being. Today, I brought a trimmer out, cut tall grass around the trailer, and tried to trim branches that were rubbing on the roof. I took a walk in the woods.

And tonight I'm smelling new mown hay.

Nothing Is Impossible

July 4, 2019
Hayward, Wisconsin

I'm not sure what to say about today.

It started badly with Dennis being up nearly every hour throughout the night for varying reasons. By morning, I felt sleep-deprived and had a headache. He was ready to be up and taken to breakfast somewhere. This was our first time leaving the trailer since Day 1, so I insisted he clean up first—shave and wash with water heated on the camp stove.

We drove into town and had a good breakfast, but had nothing to do after that, so I took him back out to the meadow. For fun (but really because I could no longer stand the mouse smell), I cleaned the skylights in the trailer. One had a nasty mouse nest in it, and I ended up taking all the screens into town with me to clean them with plentiful water. My brother tells me that we have probably stayed in the trailer longer than anyone else, and little by little, we are cleaning and fixing what we can.

Maybe I feel a little bit guilty when I leave the meadow to go into town for the day. Sometimes I come back for lunch. On days like today when we both go into town, I take him back to the meadow around noon and he stays there himself until close to dinner time. He sleeps and eats and doesn't seem to mind that there's not much else he can do.

At our condo, I enjoy modern-day pleasures such as air conditioning and running water. When I come back to the meadow in the evenings, it is the coolest time of the day and quite pleasant. Dennis seems pretty normal in his thinking and is usually moving around a little better as well.

Tonight, we warmed up some soup and sat outside, watching the meadow as we ate. A deer walked across the far end, stopping every few steps to look at us. A hawk did a circle around the meadow and landed on the top of a tall pine, probably scoping out the newly mown field for rodents. There are small birds everywhere, and the singing never goes quiet while there is light.

At times, I think Dennis realizes that he's not getting any better on a lasting basis, that there are only fluctuations, although he never voices that himself. Today he said he was glad that we had started long ago to prepare me to take over major responsibilities, like buying our vehicles, driving everywhere, making financial decisions, and pretty much planning our future. It was kind of an admission that he doesn't plan to return to those responsibilities.

At the same time, he has lately been restored to hope with the verse from the Bible about nothing being impossible for God (Matthew 19 verse 26, I think). Having just thought about that and asking for the reference in the morning, he brought it up a little later in a phone conversation with his brother, Ron. His brother was surprised when he heard that because, as he was talking with Dennis, he had been reaching into his coat pocket to remove a stone that he carried around with him. Inscribed on the stone was that very same saying: "With God nothing is impossible."

When things like this happen, they are like affirmations directly from his Heavenly Father, and they bring Dennis to tears. As they say in my online support group, LBD is a ruthless, horrible, and very sad disease. The only hope is knowing a God for whom nothing is impossible.

God's Still, Small Voice

July 11, 2019
Hayward, Our Condo

We spent two weeks living in the travel trailer in the Smith Meadow. On the Sunday we left, we made it to church and heard a sermon about Elijah. In the cave where he was resting/hiding, he heard God's still, small voice telling him to go back to a dangerous place and trust God for protection. Dennis took that to heart and said, "Let's go back to the condo."

There were other motivators, of course. He had started having difficulty keeping warm at night, to the point of feeling near-panicked. He also felt isolated and a bit afraid when he was there alone. He had started worrying about bears, although none have been reported there for quite some time. He had started thinking that there was an electric fence somewhere close that was wreaking havoc on his eyesight and his hearing. Being there was getting old and of questionable value.

We did go back to the trailer after church. I dropped him off and called a few hours later to see how he felt. "Afraid," he said. But he was feeling God wanted him to face his fears. I went out immediately and picked him up, along with a load of our most necessary stuff. We have been back in the condo now for three full days.

Symptoms have come and gone, and although he has tried to link them to high water tables, electric fields, and beaver dams being rebuilt, he is beginning to be confused as to the actual cause. Each time he starts to educate me on what he thinks is happening and runs into a wall because I cannot be convinced, he sits and prays. He renews his resolve to trust God and comes to tell me that he will try not to be afraid. He always acknowledges that being back in the modern, more convenient world is better than being in the meadow.

Yesterday we went back, briefly, to retrieve the last things from the trailer. He didn't want to go, but made himself face his fears once more. He was amazed when I told him there was no electric fence. He was amazed when he was able to step up on the deck with good balance. He was amazed when he was able to help put a few things in the truck. He was amazed when he was able to walk out of the meadow on uneven ground all the way to the main road. "This isn't really such a bad place, is it?" He said that with conviction.

No, it was nice in many ways, and I wouldn't mind coming back for a night or two now and then, which is really how I feel. In many ways, I love the meadow. It is a beautiful place to watch God's creation. But, for now, I am glad to be back to one life, in one place, one day at a time.

A Necessary Trip

July 18, 2019
Hegins, Pennsylvania

I know changes of any kind can be very upsetting, both to the elderly and to someone not feeling well, but we needed to travel. Dennis has been very emotional since his LBD diagnosis and at times feels like any moment could be his last. He has wanted to visit his hometown in Pennsylvania and see his family again one more time. I agreed.

He is also still convinced that our condo is improperly grounded and has an electric field that is killing him. He felt that two weeks on the road might make such a difference in how he felt that he would be using his computer again, doing research, reading, and working on his book project. I asked him to think about what it might mean if he didn't feel any better after time away from the condo.

"It would mean that I wasn't gone long enough. That's the logical conclusion."

So, although I will look forward to a return home at some point, he will not. He's already dreading it and doesn't hesitate to say so.

The trip to Pennsylvania went fairly well, although it was a bit like traveling with a small child when it came to getting in and out of restaurants and the motel. All things seem exaggerated to Dennis and are potentially upsetting. The 10-minute delay due to traffic conditions becomes "the most awful" part of the route, even though it was par for the course to my way of thinking. The pay stations on the toll road were "terribly stressful" and upset his stomach. Stopping for the night caused him to be so grateful for God's help in solving our problem when I wasn't aware that there was a problem—it was my plan all along.

I expected that he would feel exuberant after his first night of rest at his brother's house, but he was very quiet and wanted to go back to sleep instead of having breakfast at the hometown cafe. He had very little energy all day and fell asleep for a while, surrounded by visiting relatives and busy chatter. He cried when talking to his sister and brother, and kept thinking of things to talk about of a "final" nature.

I can see that this visit might take a lot out of him. I don't think I can do anything to help with that.

Uncomfortable Evening

July 20, 2019
Hegins, Pennsylvania

This is the fourth day of our visit to Dennis's family in Pennsylvania. It has been a good time for us overall. Today I am staying back at the house while Ron and Deanna take Dennis over to see his cousin, Jim. I have one of my three-day headaches and this is the third day, so I should be good by tomorrow. I think it might have started because they only have decaf coffee here, but I'm not sure.

But last night was interesting. It was an uncomfortable evening. Uncomfortable, but not uncommon. I think I did a fair job of not taking things too personally.

We had dinner out and were back at Ron and Deanna's house visiting—just the four of us—when Dennis started talking about his renewed plans to deal with the electricity issue. He had explained his whole theory (which to him is no longer a theory but a fact) to others during the day and was reviewing it all for his brother. As he talked about how the condo was killing him, about all his symptoms, about the people at Penn State he was going to consult with, etc... it got really weird. He talked and talked and talked, with a very flat affect, and his soft Lewy voice. We mostly just listened. Every now and then, I would give him a question to answer, to clarify some of his reporting, but I didn't say much.

And then, it got a bit more personal. He got a little agitated, talking about how we (he and I) were supposed to "be one," and he could tell I was not completely supportive of his thinking. I was not letting him have his rightful authority. He reiterated his desire to go stay with our friends in Duluth (really bad idea), only now it was for a month or more. He was pretty sure two weeks of travel was not going to be enough to bring back all his faculties. Several times, I gave the opportunity to break it off because I was wondering if his brother and his brother's wife were finding this interesting or uncomfortable. He would interrupt me and continue.

This was so uncharacteristic of Dennis, and I was getting more and more embarrassed for him. It was quite plain that he was angry with me and didn't mind accusing me of being unhelpful. I finally told him I had to go to bed, that I loved him, and that I wasn't going to stop caring for him. He quit, and they all went to bed shortly after.

I am glad it happened this way for Ron and Deanna to understand what he does that is difficult for me. To this point, Dennis's phone conversations with his brother were perhaps eccentric, but not that abnormal for Dennis. This time, I think they could see the abnormal, and how it could create strain in the relationship with me and with my mom when we were living with her.

This morning, he wanted a hug right away, and later, as he went out the door, he said he was sorry for last night.

The worst times are usually at night, and I think this is what is meant by "sundowning," perhaps? Deanna gave me a hug, too. I think it has been pretty clear to all that he has changed from his usual self in a pretty sad way.

Traveling with Lewy

July 28, 2019
Pennsylvania and North Carolina

Tomorrow we will have been gone for two weeks. No matter where we are, I am noticing new conditions that bother Dennis and need creative solutions. As a nurse, one of my most stressful jobs was with a private duty client who was always presenting me with similar challenges. I have often thought since that God was preparing me for Dennis and LBD.

In Pennsylvania, we had sleeping quarters that were somewhat small, so I opted for another room and gave Dennis the bed on the main floor close to the bathroom. The temperature regulation problem was one of the first things I noticed. There was a heat wave around the whole country at that time, and Dennis's head was getting hot all the time—only his head. He started putting a wet washcloth under his hat and wearing it most of the time. Of course, this discovery of efficient cooling had to be shared with everyone—they had to try it, and he was always telling me how everyone loved it.

The rest of his body was often cold. Since there wasn't central AC in the house, his room was warm enough at night to please him. He often complains of sweating and freezing at the same time, so it is very hard to know what to do for him.

Except for the one bad night, I did not notice big behavioral changes from previous times at home. He was often dramatic in his lectures and stories, and often weepy and emotional. It was usually in a grateful way, but toward the end of our visit, he was getting depressed, it seemed to me. He was concluding that we all were getting dementia and declining, especially his sister. Somehow, the family history of heart problems was also getting lumped in with dementia and becoming the telltale symptoms of "fatty liver disease," which he thinks is his correct diagnosis because that is familial. LBD is not familial, and the doctors wouldn't have diagnosed him that way had they known his family history. Somehow, he thinks that they skipped that part of his exam at Mayo.

Another behavioral thing I've noticed lately is that he isn't able to sit for very long, especially on hard chairs. He feels he has lost all his cushioning fat and gets sore quickly. Of course, he has even less tolerance of standing, so that leaves lying down. He does a lot of that. He was often sleepy in Pennsylvania, and much of the visiting went on around him as he slept in his chair.

Traveling On

July 24, 2019
Gibsonville, NC

We are now visiting our daughter Julie in North Carolina. The drive last Sunday was uneventful. We didn't have a heavy breakfast before we left Pennsylvania, so he wanted to stop for lunch. We pulled off the interstate and chose a place that wasn't fast food—Golden Corral. He went in and sat down. I had to load his plate for him so he wouldn't get confused with all the choices. I found a good, simple meal for him, so he was satisfied, but I noticed that he was easily confused, sleepy afterwards in the car, and anxious for the trip to be over. He's starting to think that the truck electronics are causing him to feel bad during travel. He thought it had to be the Bluetooth technology, but I told him the phone was connected by wire to the truck, so he's re-thinking that, and I'm sure he will come up with something.

Here at Julie's, he is back on what he calls his "regimen," of which magnesium is a part. He likes to do intermittent fasting in order to have periods of autophagy. He loves to use that word because then he gets to explain what it is. He wants a substantial breakfast, no lunch, and an early supper. That gives him a daytime period of autophagy and a nighttime one. Every day he tells me which things have improved. His whistle came back today. Yesterday, he wanted to know if I would celebrate with him, as he had been able to spend time on the computer and had walked outside for a few minutes as well. One day, he was excited that he had executed the complicated maneuver of setting his coffee cup on a dresser a short distance away from his chair—actually did it twice. It doesn't take much to constitute improvement.

The temperature problem is worse here. The first night in a comfortably air-conditioned room nearly froze him to death. I loved it. However, he has no trouble asking that everyone accommodate his idiosyncrasies. So, since then, we have gone without the AC and used only the fans. We also get the lecture about how moving air will make you feel cool even when you are hot. Evidently, that was supposed to surprise me. Since Julie needs her sleep, she can open a window in her room after it cools down outside. I, on the other hand, do not need to sleep in a cool room, I guess.

More Electronics

July 25, 2019
Greensboro, NC

I had to give away my piano when we left Florida, and we talked about replacing it someday with something more portable, like a nice keyboard. Since Greensboro is a fairly large city with a few music stores, I wanted to buy a keyboard while visiting there. Dennis was all for it until we were sitting in the store surrounded by all kinds of electronics. It suddenly occurred to him that a keyboard was a digital instrument with electricity involved. The sounds are not real; they are electronic reproductions. He even woke up that night very confused, saying he felt like he was not real himself and in an unfamiliar world.

I can feel him eyeing my new keyboard and getting anxious. I'm thinking I will have to refrain from using it around him and keep it covered at home, if we ever get to live at home again.

One day, I overheard him telling someone on the phone things that were actually untrue. One of the things was that the farmhouse Julie's fiancé had bought was unlivable, and was going to take all kinds of renovation before it could be lived in. It made me realize that he doesn't hear details correctly and makes wrong assumptions. Another thing was about the "fatty liver disease" he has, which made me realize that even when he's told details, he reverts to his delusions anyway. It may be his way of rebelling.

He wants to go home by way of my brother's house in Michigan, an eleven-hour travel day. This is probably what we will do, but until today, I had not verified arrangements with my brother. This morning, Dennis asked Julie to pray about us going there as he had a special reason for wanting time with my brother. I was a bit suspicious about him asking her, but not telling me, so I talked with him about it. He said it was not any of the reasons I thought, but he still has not told me what it is. I think I'm worried...

He Came Along

July 31, 2019
Gibsonville, North Carolina

Today, Dennis insisted on going with me to attend the day's work. Early yesterday morning, our 16-foot container came from the PackRat warehouse, where it has been since our move a year ago. I worked unloading all that remains of our Florida belongings into my son-in-law's basement from 10 am until 7 pm. Julie came to help around 3 pm, and Kevin came to help with the last heavier pieces of furniture. We were satisfied just to get it all into the basement. No organization whatsoever.

So, today my job was to look over everything, organize it into as small a space as possible, and identify anything we had been wanting with us in Wisconsin. I knew all of this would take time and would be easier if I were doing it myself, but Dennis wanted to come. He got ready to go quickly and was prepared to tough it out.

One of our furniture items was his mother's La-Z-Boy recliner. I cleared everything off it and made it available to him. For a while, he poked around, looking at and asking questions about furniture he didn't remember. I admit, for a man, it could be hard to recognize something that you haven't seen in a year. When he finally sat in the recliner, he remembered how much he liked it, how it didn't make his head bend too far forward, had arms at just the right height, and went back easily when he wanted to recline. I decided we would take it back to Wisconsin. (You can't believe all the different things that can be wrong about a chair until you've been around Dennis.)

I suggested he look through a trunk labeled "Dennis, memorabilia." He began to read the top layers of papers and found some interesting documents he thought he had never seen. Perhaps they were given to him years ago after his mother's funeral, when he didn't have time to go through them. There were things his mother had written and copies of her will. There was the agreement signing the family farm over to his nephew. Of course, all these brought tears and choked him up so he could hardly speak.

But the worst or best, depending on how you looked at it, was a typed-out sermon that he may or may not have actually given. He didn't remember giving it, and it was so long that he couldn't imagine having been given time to deliver it either. It was basically the story of his life, particularly his spiritual development and his time in the Worldwide Church of God. Reading his decisions made years ago, I heard him say things like, "I was so wrong back then." And "I still have questions about that." He wrote about his relationships with significant people in his life. He cried, reading it out loud to me as I worked. He was such an emotional mess that I had to go hunting for some tissues for his eyes and nose. He was pretty exhausted when he finished.

The funny thing is that he didn't mention wanting the chest to go back to Wisconsin with us. He read only a few things in the top layer. When it was time to leave, I closed it up and stacked it with our other things in storage. It stays there in Kevin's basement.

He's had a persistent train of thought that significant family items should be given to his brother or to his nephews, almost like he's forgotten that he has daughters who are going to want something from his side of the family. There are pieces of furniture and some very old coins that were given to him. I'm pretty sure he wants his girls to make decisions about those things, and I'm going to make sure that is what happens.

Loading the truck with the chair and quite a few other precious things was challenging, especially trying to get my new keyboard in the cab with us, where it would be cooler. Dennis had all kinds of suggestions, and he did try to help. We struggled, loaded and reloaded a couple of times, and I finally called it quits, with the keyboard sticking out the open window of the back seat. We strapped ourselves in, only to discover that the keys were nowhere to be found. I was afraid they were in the back seat, underneath everything. Mind you, it was about 90 degrees in the shade, and we were very tired.

I unloaded everything in the back seat one more time, asking God for help, as I almost always do for everything I lose. I was not seeing them and about to do something desperate, when Dennis, the person who never finds anything, found the keys. He happened to see my purse on the floor on his side of the cab and looked in a pocket that I had not searched and seldom used. They were there.

How wonderful he felt to be used by God in a very unaccustomed role. We do what we can, but it is God who chooses us and equips us for what is needed. It made a nice resolution to a very frustrating time. I was happy for him, and for myself.

PART FOUR: CONTINUING THE SEARCH

Running Out Ahead

August 3, 2019
Gibsonville, NC

The husband keeps repenting of "running out ahead" of God. He is a problem solver, and problems drive him crazy—it always seems to him that because he is aware of the problem, it is his to solve. He is not comfortable waiting for God. It's usually in retrospect that he realizes his "running ahead."

I am not saying that I condone inaction, waiting on everything because one is too lazy to address issues. That drives me crazy. When a problem is there to be solved, I am willing to pray about it and do whatever comes to mind in a reasonable fashion. Do something, do one thing and see what happens next...

Lately, almost daily, new problems are coming up on Dennis's radar. He thinks about them obsessively. When there isn't an actual problem, he thinks of a possible problem. He comes to me three or four times in the space of an hour, with more to say about the developing structure of the problem. It grows, takes shape in his mind, and is often described as a dangerous situation, not just to him but to others as well. He must figure out what to do and intervene. He must convince others that action is required because he is not physically capable of doing what is needed by himself. What a dilemma. His world has a lot of anxiety in it.

The basement where his stuff is stored is likely going to flood because there are springs on the property.

The coming trip back home is dreaded because something in the truck is messing with his eyesight and making him sleepy. His wife, who is driving, will fall asleep, and there will be an accident.

He has heard that the A/C in his daughter's house hasn't been serviced in the two years she's lived here. Danger, danger...

He might run out of vitamins or pineapple on the trip home and his whole health regimen will go down the tubes.

There must be a reason he's had the word "Fabian" given (by God) to him to investigate. Who is Fabian Farrington, and how can he discover why he needs to know?

How can he keep from being further brain-damaged while his wife is using the hotspot to access the internet?

How can he convince the code officials of the need to reverse their thinking about grounding rods in duplexes? People's lives are at stake.

Who wouldn't be anxious? It seems to me that the challenge is to be aware of possible problems AND aware that someone more capable than one's self is working out the solution. Trust someone else. Trust God. Learn to wait without stressing out. Like the sign I saw yesterday in the barn I was in: "Remember stressed, spelled backward, is dessert." Yes it is, just sayin'...

"Search me, O God, and know my heart; test me and know my anxious thoughts" Psalm 139:23.

Because I Can

August 18, 2019
Hayward, WI

I have to say that I am relieved. We have had nearly two weeks at home that have been relatively stable. Dennis is doing so many things that seem different than the usual LBD heaviness, not that it is all gone, but he feels better much of the time. That makes it easier for him to think, converse, and go places. He watches TV, eats regular meals, and sleeps at night for the most part.

Last night he came in, puffing and panting and looking a bit haggard. He said he had just run on his usual walking route. I asked him why he ran, and he said, "Because I can."

Okay. This is the guy who would hardly walk more than a few feet two weeks ago. He's decided that he should push himself to exercise, knowing that he will not want to do it, but should for the benefits it provides. He decided he should learn where the dishes get put away in the kitchen so he could help with cleaning up. He's been shaving himself and doing a much better job of it.

His vision is still pretty bad, he still has some obsessions with how he's feeling and reports almost minute by minute—his whistle is gone, or his bathroom time didn't go well, or he has no feeling on the right side of his face—stuff like that. Every now and then, he worries about the electricity thing, that it will come back again when the water table rises. But overall, he is doing so much better that it gives me a much more pleasant life. I cook meals, garden, fix the condo up a bit, visit with my mom and brother's family, take walks and bike rides by myself. I feel somewhat normal, even with the limitations of our situation.

Once, last week, we loaded up the lounge chair and went out to Round Lake. I set him up near the water at the boat landing, where he could watch people and boats. He even shelled peas while he was there, although I would not give him the job again unless he gets a little faster at it. I was able to take a long walk and swim before we came back home. It was a lovely afternoon. I want to do it again.

The question I have is, "How long will this last?" It's an evil disease, from what I hear from others. We have been blessed so far that he has not been so confused as to get violent, has not had hallucinations, and has not been so debilitated that he couldn't move, eat, speak, etc...

We've been dealt a merciful hand, and I am grateful.

Disappointment

August 25, 2019
Hayward, WI

As I have written, he decided to run because he could. Well, it seems that he shouldn't have assumed that he could, because there were consequences.

His back became really painful as his muscles responded to the "running," which made him remember the chiropractor and how long it had been since he'd gone for an adjustment. We went twice last week, and he got enough relief each time that he was very impressed with the chiropractor and how much he knew. Still, he had problems that returned each night as he slept.

I say "slept," but I'm starting to wonder if he does get much sleep. He tells me in the morning that he has been awake to go to the bathroom nearly every hour. He no sooner gets back in bed than he has to go again. It's almost like the act of lying horizontal causes him to feel the need.

This morning, when I came to ask if he was up and getting prepared to go to church, he definitely was not. Every movement of getting out of bed, trying to walk with the cane, sitting, standing again—it was all so slow and guarded that there was no way he could go anywhere. He does not tolerate pain well. So our plans for the day took an about-face.

Not only did we stay home from church, but we also cancelled dinner out with friends because he could not get dressed, ride in the car, or wait for a table. He did not want to be left alone at home either. It's not that he will allow me to help him or touch him; he just wants someone to stand by if needed and to listen to him talk about all his calculations about how to move or why he can't make a certain movement. I have to keep reminding myself that he can't help it. It's the disease.

This is a disappointing setback in our stretch of fairly stable days. I know it's a bit selfish, but I also really wanted to go out to dinner...

Mattresses, Temp, Hair

September 6, 2019
Hayward, WI

It has been a week since I last asked myself how we are doing. Funny how it is easier not to do that too often, as it could lead to incredibly sad thoughts.

Dennis still thinks he is getting better, or at least holding steady. I think he is doing okay cognitively, but his motor problems are still there and worsening some. We can sit and have fairly reasonable conversations. He is able to talk about his condition without as much denial, although he still has to try to figure everything out—every new symptom, every change in the old symptoms, figure, figure, figure...

Since returning from the meadow to the condo, he has tried many different sleeping arrangements in search of the perfect, comfortable night. He never quite arrives there.

For a while, he slept in the master bedroom, but immediately there were issues with the bed being too high. We have different temperature preferences as well, so I would end up sleeping in a recliner in the living room just to keep cool.

He moved to the guest room, and for a while, I thought we had a good thing going there, but no. Soon the mattress was too soft, and he couldn't turn over. There was no solid surface to push against.

The search for a firmer mattress took him back to the master bedroom. It also has a smaller twin bed that he slept in several nights before he began to be uncomfortable. He had his back injury by this time and had difficulty getting in and out or moving at all. He would lie on one side only all night, and that side was getting sore. But the smaller bed gave him no room to turn around without hitting the wall. He also was noticing the amount of drag that his clothing gave on the sheets. Every time he tried to turn, he would either lose his blanket completely or get tangled up in it.

Next, he remembered an offer of a firmer mattress to exchange for the one in the guest room. My brother and I hauled the mattresses back and forth, and surprisingly, it resulted in a lower bed and a firmer mattress. I thought it would be perfect. He practiced rolling from one side to the other. He measured the distance to get his feet up on the bed, and the distance he sank down when sitting on the side (he does this on all beds now—the firmness test).

Having discovered the blanket problem, he has now decided to sleep without them. This is when he started measuring the temperature of various parts of the room with his infrared thermometer. It was too cold for sleeping without covers. We had to get a small heater, which we did. Keeping the door closed was also necessary to keep the heat in so, for safety's sake, we had to get a monitor so I could hear him when he needed help.

It took several nights of trying the heater in different places—a chair was too high and made the floor cold and the ceiling too hot. The air wasn't mixing right. He is still a physicist and cannot be in situations like this without reverting to his lifelong career. He has to figure out why air goes where it goes. This morning after getting up, he asked me to go into his "incubator" and measure the temps—80 degrees F on the ceiling, 78 pretty much everywhere else. Perfect. You would think.

Another spin-off from his "out of whack" heating and cooling system is his desire for longer hair. Winter is coming, and his head will certainly get cold. He has resisted having it cut, and also doesn't want to shave his facial hair. He was looking quite shaggy and unkempt the other day when we went into Dairy Queen to buy a couple dinners. He sat down to wait while I fixed our drinks, which I put in the truck. I told him he could go out and get seated, and I would wait and bring the food when it was ready. He went out. The people at a nearby table were concerned and about to follow him out and bring him back, since his appearance and way of moving signaled that he was obviously not all right in the head. They were afraid he was running away and would get lost. Wow.

The good news is that today I convinced him to get a haircut. My nephew has recently started working at a barbershop in town, and I framed the outing as a chance to encourage a young person in their career. That is definitely something that Dennis responds to these days. It gives him purpose and a way to connect with someone other than his wife—me. I'm also grateful for that. He looks pretty spiffy now, hair cut and beard trimmed. Definitely worth the price.

Finding Hope

September 9, 2019
Hayward, WI

I am excited to learn that what is happening in LBD is really the body's attempt to defend itself. God has designed us marvelously, and if we treat our bodies right, they will heal themselves. Sometimes, that is the miracle.

Originally, my hope was that God would help us through whatever was ahead with Lewy body dementia, or maybe even heal Dennis of it completely. I thought a miraculous healing was the only way that would happen. The medical specialists we encountered gave no other hope from their side of things. I was even a little shocked that, having been given the diagnosis and a prescription for a drug that could maybe help cognitive function for "a little while," we were dismissed with no recommendation for follow-up of any kind.

Dennis did some research shortly after that, which started him on a different track. He believed, or wanted desperately to believe, that he was going to turn this disease around. Several things made him think that, one of which was a report that claimed cognitive decline in Alzheimer's dementia had been reversed in a small study. The patients involved responded to the therapy and regained what they had lost, went back to work and normal functioning.

Since then, the researcher, a UCLA-based physician, has written a book, *The End of Alzheimer's*, detailing the therapy. He also shares the story of how the research progressed to develop a new understanding of cognitive decline in neurodegenerative diseases. I love this quote from the book:

"Now, often the most interesting and revealing experiments—the moments when an invisible chemical or an inconsequential cell can move the Earth—are not the ones that succeed as expected, nor are they the ones that fail outright: they are the ones that yield results that are just the opposite of what you expected."[2]

I can feel his excitement from the beginning of his search right up to the present. Hundreds of people have benefited from this protocol, which has been named ReCode, and word is spreading quickly, thanks more to the web than anything else. Dr. Dale Bredesen and those who have gotten their life back after Alzheimer's have a passion for conquering this devastating disease.

I have finished most of the book, finally. We have had it for some time, but there have been so many things to cope with, so many surprises, so many caretaking problems to solve, that I have been overwhelmed. Fortunately, we have already been learning about and doing some of the things in the protocol. Even though I was skeptical of some of Dennis's practices of magnesium supplementation, of autophagy, and his extremes of fasting and avoiding electricity, we have been doing a lot of it. Maybe that has been responsible for slowing further decline.

I am hopeful. Everyone should know about this, because Alzheimer's, Parkinson's, LBD, and other dementias are becoming ep-

---

2 Bredesen, Dale E. *The End of Alzheimer's: The First Program to Prevent and Reverse Cognitive Decline*. Avery, 2017.

idemic and they can be prevented, according to Dr. Bredesen. As Bredesen and his researchers agree, no one should die like this, and they don't have to. Reading the book gave me a little more hope.

Functional Medicine

September 17, 2019
Hayward, WI

Some things are so complex that they must be digested in small portions. That is what I'm feeling now, since reading *The End of Alzheimer's.*

Dennis has been questioning why we aren't rushing down to the medical lab in Eau Claire and having him tested so he can begin the reversal process on his LBD. Last night I followed up on the tests recommended in the book—some 50 of them, each costing from $100 to $300. It was difficult to tell if the lab offered the specific tests that we would want. It was also difficult to know which should be done first, or if some were more important than others. It was above my pay scale to figure it all out. Which led me to the recommendation to search out a functional medicine doctor.

I really like the direction functional medicine is taking. I ended up watching an hour-long lecture by a doctor at Cleveland Clinic. He was explaining functional medicine, where it started, and why it was needed. I totally agree. It has added another very complex area of information to consider in the battle to save Dennis's brain.

I will not take the time to explain what functional medicine is, except to say that we are seeing the results in the medical news when we hear about inflammation being the root of so many chronic diseases. That comes from discoveries in functional medicine. Also, the new emphasis on our microbiome and the problem of "leaky gut." That also comes out of functional medicine research. These doctors are interested in the root cause of chronic conditions. They are aware that each patient has different reasons for becoming ill, and different remedies are needed. Good stuff.

I tried to give a simple picture to Dennis—why we are not rushing into the lab work. The good news is that there is a functional medicine practitioner in our health network. The office is 90 miles from us, but we are used to going that far for specialists. I'm hoping we can make an appointment and get help sorting through the complexity of testing.

Meanwhile, I'm pretty sure we've been doing some of the right things in the magnesium supplementation and the ketogenic diet (which we need to follow a bit more closely...). Dennis is feeling and acting better. We do not know if it is in response to what we are doing or just a fluctuation of LBD. Time will tell. At any rate, things are better right now, and I, for one, am enjoying that part of it.

Just Enjoy It

September 24, 2019
Hayward, WI

We have been in a pretty pleasant place for several weeks now. There have been no big changes, no unusual delusions or fears—just a slow and steady movement toward a routine and a "new normal" life.

It has allowed me time to finish the garden and do some canning and freezing. I've become more regular at cooking meals and even sharing mealtime with family once or twice a week. I've bought a few things for the house, which some people call "nesting," and we've settled into our two bedrooms. It works fine to separate us at night, since we like different temperatures and wake at different times. I get much better sleep this way. This is all possible because Dennis's back pain has resolved, and he is able to manage himself by himself. He is able to get in and out of bed, adjust his own blankets, and get to the bathroom without my help.

Also, another delusion was discarded yesterday. It has started to bother him recently that he misses so much of any conversation. He was investigating buying new hearing aids of the old analog style, ones that wouldn't be beaming microwave radiation into his head. Somehow, he convinced himself that the tube going into his ear was just a sound tube (which it is) and that it was perfectly safe to put his old hearing aids back in. Some articles I've read do express concern about the small amount of EMF emitted by the part of the hearing aid worn behind the ear because they are worn for so many hours every day. I am not directing him to those articles.

He reads a little bit again. He watches TV a lot—only shows that don't upset him. He takes short walks without the cane or walker, eats his meals without trouble, and has been much easier to converse with. He seems a little more aware of his appearance. His blood pressure has been lower on a regular basis. All this is good, and we will enjoy it as long as it lasts.

Is any of this due to taking magnesium, following a largely keto diet, and being healthier? Is it a slow healing in answer to prayer? Is it only a fluctuation in the course of LBD? I don't really know and am wondering. Time will tell.

A Problem Walk

October 2, 2019
Hayward, WI

After several weeks of stability and no new problems developing, I was surprised by what happened today.

Dennis decided he should go for a walk. It's been cold and rainy, making it easy to stay inside without really planning to avoid exercise. He realized his walks had been infrequent. He also has had trouble sleeping and staying asleep and thought the exercise might improve that problem.

I noticed right from the beginning that he was walking slowly. He had to be reminded every few steps to pick up his feet and walk instead of shuffle. We got to our turnaround point and he began to lean to his right and couldn't straighten up. The steps got shorter, and he said he had to stop for a minute.

I thought his posture might be making it more difficult to walk because at this point, he was leaning back and to the side, with his belly thrust forward and his knees always bent. It was very strange, and he couldn't correct it, but he insisted on "walking it out." A few steps later, he was locking up and hardly able to move, so I ran back to the house for the walker with the sit-down option. He tried to walk with it, but soon gave up and sat down. He pushed himself backward, seated in the walker, all the way to the house. He even had trouble with that. It was very odd.

He was also puzzled, but decided that he had gone too far and had simply gotten tired. He was glad to be back in the house, resting in a chair that he could easily get up from.

This whole episode was very Parkinsonian in nature. I have thought that perhaps he was getting better, reversing some of his symptoms affecting mood and cognition. That may still be the case, but this is a setback toward a movement disorder. It's unsettling to me. I have been counting on him being able to move himself. If he loses that ability, I don't know if I can care for him without more help. This is not feeling good.

Deep Vein Thrombosis

November 1, 2019
Hayward, WI

This morning, Dennis met me in the hall as I was going over to check on Mom. He said his leg felt funny during the night when he woke up—not exactly painful, but swollen and harder. I felt it and agreed that it was slightly larger and warmer to the touch. It was worth sending a note to the doctor through the health app, and they messaged back that he should be seen in the clinic. He got in by 11 am, and they decided to check for deep vein thrombosis, DVT, with an ultrasound of his leg. We were walking over to radiology when he got faint, sweaty, and couldn't go further. I got him a wheelchair, and we made it to the ultrasound. He felt better by then, so the tech did the procedure while I watched.

They saw an extensive DVT and sent him to the ER right away. I was impressed with the number of people who practically mobbed him. He was hooked up to all the monitors in no time flat. The ER doc sent him for a CT scan of the lungs, and it showed multiple emboli in both lungs. So it wasn't long before he was put on anticoagulants and admitted to the hospital. The whole ordeal sent his blood pressure sky high, too, so he was put back on medicine for that as well.

Pineapple Therapy

November 17, 2019
Hayward, WI

He stayed in the hospital for two days and was discharged. Although he seems more tired and weaker than usual, his cognition has seemed better. He stands and walks like a very old man, his right hand is afflicted with a persistent tremor, and everything he does is slow, slow, and slower.

He had a follow-up appointment this week and when getting ready, he was commending himself for showering and dressing himself without help. Is he getting somewhat more independent? Maybe.

From time to time, he puzzles over his "words" that he is sure God has given him, and tries to reassure himself that he hasn't made them up. A couple of days ago he had an "aha!" moment over the word "proteolytic." God brought it to his awareness some time ago, and ever since, he has responded by eating pineapple at every meal. Pineapple was the only available food that had a proteolytic enzyme. Still, he hadn't quite figured out why God wanted him to do that, until now.

It was brought to his attention after the CT scan that he had some sort of mass showing on his stomach, which will need to be addressed after he is done with the anticoagulants. He started thinking maybe there would be a connection to proteolytic enzymes, and sure enough, he found an article where someone's stomach cancer had been eradicated with bromelain, an enzyme in pineapple. So, God had him working on his stomach, eating pineapple and taking proteolytic enzymes way before he even knew he needed them. He's expecting the mass to be gone by the time it's investigated.

He is not exactly at the place where I feel he would be safe alone at home. He doesn't find things easily, including food and clothes, so it might be awkward if I left for any length of time longer than a few hours. I cancelled my trip to NC for a writing conference and watched it online instead. Maybe if he had to take care of himself, he would rise to the challenge, but I think it would be hard on him. I think it's going to be a long winter with a lot of staying home for us.

The Awaited Meeting

December 4, 2019
Duluth, MN

Today was the long-awaited appointment with the functional medicine practitioner.

Dennis was very excited about the book *End to Alzheimer's* by Bredesen and wanted to find a doctor who would put him on that protocol. The book pointed us to a website of functional medicine doctors, and lo, one of the ones listed was in our medical group.

Armed with all his records and having filled out numerous detailed questionnaires, we made the 90-mile trip to Duluth for our morning appointment. Dr. Nancy Sudak, who wants to be called Nan, is also a family medicine practitioner. She was a middle-aged woman who actually took Dennis's blood pressure herself. And if that wasn't enough to single her out as a different kind of doctor, she then spent 90 minutes chatting with us! As with other times when I have listened to Dennis recount his journey with this illness, I wondered how long she would let him go on. She was carefully sizing him up in areas other than physical. Functional medicine means taking everything into account. However, she finally had to tell Dennis to stop his stories and let her get to pertinent facts (in a kind, respectful way).

We liked her demeanor, and she was patient with Dennis. She did allow him to talk about his spirituality and his words from God without making him feel demeaned or demented. At the conclusion of the interview, she even approached the subject of needed changes by asking him to ask God about the changes. Would God want him to consider going gluten-free or dairy-free in his diet? I thought that was pretty clever.

She also had heard of Dr. Bredesen's protocol and was interested in it. She ordered some of the pertinent tests which we remembered from the book (GI map, bloodwork). She was also able to recognize the measures Dennis had already implemented and encouraged him in them.

Overall, it was a good start. The only disappointment was that she had basically nothing to recommend until the test results returned and couldn't give another appointment until February. It will be a teleconference next time, so we won't have to go so far.

December Update

December 21, 2019
Hayward, WI

Thanksgiving has come and gone. December is almost over as well. This is our second winter since the diagnosis, and I was thinking over the past year and comparing our present with the past.

Dennis is thinner, less physically active, and a bit more dependent, but not drastically changed. I think I notice Parkinsonian symptoms increasing faster than anything else. His hand trembles almost all the time when he isn't holding something or doing some motion. His face is rather mask-like, and his voice is soft, monotone, and often hard to distinguish. He always shuffles now, especially outside when he's trying not to slip on snow or ice, but also in the house. And he is sooo sloooow.

Since the hospitalization last month, he has not had any trouble with thrombosis—but, of course, he is on an anticoagulant. The doctor says he may have to stay on it indefinitely. He has had continuing trouble with his blood pressure being high, and we are still working on getting that stabilized.

He has been much more content to stay at home by himself. He watches a lot of TV, takes naps, talks on the phone to anyone who answers his calls, and does a lot of thinking. I'm never sure what he is thinking about, but he's awake and has on his "thinking face." I'll bet he's wondering if he's ever going to be well. Yesterday, I felt it was safe to leave him at home alone while I took Mom to the doctor for outpatient surgery. He found his own breakfast and lunch without having to call me, which is an accomplishment for him.

One thing we have added lately is a membership in the senior fitness program at the hospital. He uses the stationary bike when we are there, usually for 30 minutes, and then he is done. I have to instigate our trips there, and I intended to be faithful at that, but no, I haven't done so well.

December is his birthday month. In fact, his day is the day after Christmas, which means it's always felt a little anticlimactic. It's a good thing he doesn't have expectations of grandeur. We usually have to remind him that it's his birthday. This year, both daughters are coming to celebrate with us. They have been faithful visitors since the diagnosis of Lewy body dementia. He will not have a hard time enjoying them, since he is still quite good cognitively. I got him a couple of things, too, but I cannot say what they are because I want them to be a surprise.

The thing that disturbs me most lately is that I feel emotionally distanced from him. I don't know if it's my problem or his or a combination. Some days I spend time reading to him and that seems good, or I take him to exercise and to lunch, also good. But a lot of days, I would rather spend my time elsewhere. His interests and topics of conversation are very limited and not very interesting to me. I feel like he talks at me, not with me. Once he starts, it's hard to get him to stop, and I often just walk away without him seeming to notice at all. He just keeps talking. I seldom want to watch TV with him. I'm thankful I have a room to retreat to, where I can read or talk on the phone or watch a movie. I know I'm neglecting his social well-being, but I am not sorry enough to do something about it.

I have asked him to think about what he wants to do for our anniversary in mid-January. He isn't saying much.

Fathers and Daughters

January 3, 2020
Hayward, Wisconsin

Who ever thought we would live this long?

Dennis had his 74th birthday a little over a week ago. Both of our daughters made the trip to be with him. They are always mindful now that each trip could be the last time for them to see their dad. Even though that is always the case with all of us, we take it more seriously when there is a diagnosis, a known cause for demise.

His birthday gifts included a boom box, which he now uses to play his audio CDs, a masculine neck chain with a cross, which he had expressed interest in having, and a 23andMe kit to get his DNA tested. Oh, and steak knives to help cut all that tough meat that I serve him... He was pleased with it all. Instead of cake, he wanted pie, and he got it.

I think we all enjoyed the time together. I asked the girls what changes they saw in Dennis. I think they both noticed a weight loss, but not much else. He was even-tempered, thinking fairly well, and able to be present in all the activities we did inside. None of us stayed up late or partied hard. We tried to get outside as much as we could, and that's where Dennis declined, staying in to watch TV or take a nap. I did feel like we left him alone a number of times, but he didn't say that he minded.

He has immersed himself in the viewpoints of his favorite TV speakers. That did get him into trouble once when conversing with his youngest, who had to point out to him that there might be differing ways of looking at things. I think this little tense moment might have been even worse if it had happened a couple of years ago. His condition has actually mellowed him somewhat—he is less sure of himself, and maybe more humble. He did not wish to antagonize and got past it quite well, I thought.

There are always uncertain moments when he wants to speak in public, which he does not shy away from. I never know what he is going to say, although it is usually something I have already heard him say at home. He is thinking all the time, trying to analyze his dreams and the different events that fill his days. He is always remarking about how bizarre things seem to him. I am always remarking on how awkward things seem to me.

By the grace of God, Dennis is still physically mobile, although very cautious and slow. He hasn't lost control of any bodily functions either. He is still bothered by the hand tremor, and his voice is often weak and wispy, but everything else is pretty much like a normal old man (a very old man).

Activities which he is able to enjoy include exercising at the hospital gym, which has also provided some new interesting friends and some good lunches at the bistro. I read to him often, and he is able to stay wakeful and interested for long periods of time. And just today I showed him the karaoke app on my iPad and had him sing a number of songs. I think that might help strengthen his voice, and he did pretty well at it.

What more can I say? I think we are doing well.

Anniversary 47

January 11, 2020
Hayward, WI

Anniversaries are for reminding us of truths that keep us going, just sayin'...

Five years ago, on January 11, 2015, I sat writing as I am now, on the same subject—the wedding anniversary coming up in a couple of days. I took a picture of my diamond and thought about all it meant to me, being married for forty-two years.

The ring looks a lot different now. Since it no longer fit me, I had the diamond reset. My preference changed to white gold somewhere in the last thirty years, and I worried about the prongs wearing off and losing the stone. The price of the gold in the old ring wasn't enough to pay for the new one, so it cost me. I could only afford to replace the engagement ring with the stone in a secure beveled setting, but it was good to be able to wear it again.

The new setting suits me. It is plain, safe. It doesn't collect garden dirt or catch on my sweaters. It fits, although I don't know for how long. My hands keep... growing.

Life has changed. We are changing with it. It's been a little over a year since my husband got his diagnosis of Lewy body dementia. That day wasn't when the problem started, but it did mark the change in his focus. How does one think about anything else when faced with a prognosis like that? His world has gotten smaller in so many ways, limited in large part by his dependence on me.

Today, at home, he was relatively quiet while we ate a meal with some friends and listened to a sermon on the internet. He spent most of the day in his recliner in the corner of the living room, looking very tired. He asked me once what I was doing. He went to bed early.

It means a lot to me that he is not ungrateful. He is not a big complainer. He puts up with me dusting him off all the time and fixing his clothing. He eats what I fix for meals and tells me when it is good. He willingly follows my suggestions. He sits still while I trim his beard. He doesn't get mad when I easily do the things that are hard for him. He doesn't criticize my decisions about money or schedules. He is still here, a sweet person, a nice guy, thinking, trying to manage his daily existence as much as he can. But there is very little that he can contribute to us, to our marriage, to our future. His executive functioning is not working well.

Most of the time, I cannot imagine what he thinks about. I even have trouble describing my own feelings about what has happened to us. For our anniversary, should I not be able to put words to what's meaningful for us?

It is for times like this that we make promises to each other. Our marriage vows had the old-fashioned words "in sickness and in health, till death parts us." We had no idea who would be sick; no one does, usually. Few have the ability to think about what that means when the excitement of marriage and all it entails is new. But now, forty-seven years later, the promises have become meaningful. It means that we own these new circumstances together.

Now it makes sense to me what covenant marriage is. There were three of us making promises on the day Dennis and I married. God, who heard my promises, now helps me to keep them. God, who knows all about grief, loss, dread, panic, and everything else I experience, finds ways to support me. He assures me that promises kept will be worth it and that growing in personal integrity will be satisfying and rewarding. Our days now are preparing us for something bigger and better in the future. They are not the end!

So, on Tuesday the 14th, I will remind the husband that he is not alone. I am keeping him company as long as I am able, and I'm going to do my best to keep life from being dull. I guess he kind of does that for me, too. There are gifts all around us that we can point out to each other. Maybe that's how we'll spend our "Happy Anniversary."

Ahead of the Science

February 13, 2020
Hayward, WI

I have not updated for a month. It has been a relatively quiet time lately, and I hope it continues for several more months, if not for the duration. We are getting pretty good at living with things the way they are now.

Today we did very little except visit the local clinic. Dennis has been feeling good, he says, but then he doesn't deal with pain, so he seldom has real complaints. He hasn't had dizzy spells or been confused lately. Last week, he walked almost every day at the hospital. But this morning, he had trouble feeling normal. His ears felt clogged, and sounds in his head, like his own voice, were uncomfortably loud. He said his swallowing was problematic. So it was a good day to visit a doctor.

Our first appointment was a teleconference from the clinic with the functional medicine doctor in another city. We were there at 10:15, but there were computer problems. Two hours and three nurses later, none of whom could solve the problem, we left. They told us to check back with teleconferencing when we returned in the afternoon for a visit to our primary doctor.

We did get something done during the time at home between appointments. We both took a nap. Naps are wonderful because not only are we doing something about being tired, but we also are not making any extra work for ourselves while we're sleeping. Win, win.

We had a good bit of news when talking with the primary doc. Dennis gets to stop taking the blood thinner—the one that costs $500 for a month's supply. However, now that he is going off that med, he is clear to have an investigation of the stomach mass that was seen on the scan in November. So now he is scheduled to have an upper GI endoscopy on Monday. They use propofol, which isn't reputed to give problems to LBD patients. They might be able to get a biopsy through this means, and it was the easiest first thing to do.

The computer problems were solved when we checked in with the teleconference room, so we were able to spend 45 minutes with the functional medicine doctor that we missed in the morning. She went over some test results with us and recommended that Dennis go gluten-free and start several new supplements. Overall, she was very pleased with the test results, especially the lipid profile and A1c. Apparently, he's healthy as a horse (I searched for a better analogy... didn't work). We walked one circle in the hospital halls afterwards and then went home.

I don't know what to say about Dennis. What I do say seems like a broken record. He still gets tired easily. He goes to sleep early, wakes up late, and takes naps. He sits most of the time, either looking at his phone or the TV. He's very slow in most movements, since he is usually thinking about something else, or trying to be very careful. I am so used to his slow pace that I can't tell if it's getting worse or not. Occasionally, he can go faster if he thinks there's a reason or if he panics, but then, he's never been a person in a hurry. His right hand tremor is still there, and he thinks it's starting in his left as well.

In spite of the problems, he has been remarkably calm, self-controlled, and capable of taking care of himself for hours at a time. He still has a simplistic view of human physiology and is always researching new ways to clear the amyloid proteins out of his brain. He thinks there should be some simple, common substance that he can take to scrub his brain clean. The latest attempt is to take black cohosh, which he thinks is a natural source of secretase, a proteolytic enzyme. I've tried to convince him otherwise—no luck.

He loves to think about spiritual things and enjoys our time reading the Bible and having devotions. He's very concerned about others, especially our sister-in-law who has cancer, and he prays for them. He talks mostly about the things he's seen on TV, even when others don't seem to be interested, so he's still not very aware. One other thing I notice is that his voice is always soft and breathy, like his throat is swollen. It makes me hurt to listen to him, and I often have to ask him to repeat. His speech is flat and without vocal variety.

He wants, with all his heart, to believe that he is reversing his condition by the things he is doing and that Dr. Bredesen's treatment of Alzheimer's is working for him as well. I imagine it was disappointing for him to hear Dr. Sudak say that he was a little "ahead of the science"—that is, if he really heard it.

He Knows

February 13, 2020
Hayward, WI

At the breakfast table, he said, "I just can't wait until I can go out and mow the lawn, get my driver's license back, go shopping and use my credit card..."

I did not say anything until later, when I reminded him that he could use his credit card any time we were in the store.

"I know," he said. It's funny the things people miss.

Going Backwards

February 25, 2020
Hayward, WI

Is this going to be the end of our half-year of stability? I hope not, but things do seem to be getting a little weird lately. I really think the protocol the husband has been on has done good for him, so it will be a disappointment if we run into trouble again. Going backwards is not fun.

In November, when he had a blood clot in his leg, he was put back on blood pressure medicines because he was very hypertensive. An additional one was added a month or so later because he was still running high. Well, his readings started coming down, and then he began having times when it was low enough that he would feel dizzy and weak. I took away the diuretic, and that helped somewhat. Now it is low more often and we have started cutting the last blood pressure med in half. This is how Lewy body dementia plays with the autonomic nervous system, and it's why they call it a "roller coaster."

He has also noticed more hand tremor, and it is affecting both hands now. Because all this is worrisome to him, he has started back on his research in earnest. That, and watching all his favorite TV preachers every day, keeps him quite occupied. He is still thinking logically, and his temperament is good, but things could change for the worse. I'm so hoping NOT because...

I'm taking some time away in March to be with my daughter in Seattle. My brother Gary and his girlfriend Lyn are coming to stay in the house with Dennis. I've assured them that he doesn't need actual care, just some oversight and help with meals and questions about where things are. Nothing about travel is easy here in remote northwest Wisconsin. With the arrangements I had to make to get to the airport, Dennis will end up being by himself for about a day and a half before Gary arrives. There are others who can look in on him. I'm counting on this to be okay.

At first, I planned that we might both go on the trip. Dennis was surprised, and I could see some anxiety as he tried to adjust to the plan. When I told him he didn't have to go, he was somewhat disappointed, but also pleased that I thought he was well enough to stay home without me. I don't think the thought of staying home is making him anxious. I could be wrong.

New things include some fancy probiotics and liposomal glutathione, which the functional medicine doctor has prescribed. Correcting what is happening in the gut is very important to her. We are also giving "gluten-free" a trial. The dining room table has a growing collection of bottles and containers now, which I'm not too happy about, but it's too much trouble to put it all away in between uses.

I should get him walking/exercising again. We did so well for a week or two, and then we started having to avoid germs and being around people with colds. We have a family member in cancer treatment who has low immunity. I know we can't stop living normally—she wouldn't want that—but at the same time, it would be awful to be the ones causing a dangerous infection of some kind.

All for now. Can it be that spring is almost here?

Our Special Station

March 16, 2020
Hayward, WI

I'm confused. I don't know whose brain is having the most trouble anymore—mine or his. Is he getting better? Sometimes I think so, but it's never clear enough for me to start treating him like he's becoming more capable. And I think that's making him angry, in a very suppressed, passive-aggressive way. It's not very much fun.

Our special station is TBN, Trinity Broadcasting Network. There are some very good shows on it, and I love seeing what is going on in the world with missions and Christian initiative. But it's on almost all our waking hours, and probably 80% of it is preaching, one speaker after another. You know that cadence of voice that is associated with preaching—yeah, that's it. Almost all of them talk that way, and I say "talk" in a general way, because a lot of the time it's yelling. There's always some man on a stage yelling at a huge auditorium full of people. I don't always feel like I'm getting more of God via TBN. I feel like I'm getting more of preachers.

Another thing that they all do is ask for money to sustain their ministry. Of course, they have bills, and they are doing work for God. The husband is very soft-hearted and convicted by all the yelling. He wants to give them money, maybe not all of them, but many and often. He's been watching them for months, knows their jokes, their speaking habits, what their wives look like, and how many children they have. They are his friends, so when they ask, he wants to respond.

Just today, he told me he really wanted to get a certain book, which comes with a $40 donation. Another preacher talks about how he has a habit of carrying hundred dollar bills around and handing them out when the Lord tells him to. The husband would love to be that man. He doesn't carry money in his wallet anymore, and I wonder if he's subconsciously afraid he might give it all away if he did.

Not too long ago, in his musing about how wonderful it would be when he got well, he mentioned that it would be so much fun to go to the store and buy something himself. I reminded him, once again, that he had a credit card in his wallet and could do that now if he wanted to. This time, he seemed surprised.

He thinks he might be well this summer and should be able to ride his bike. It must be hard to have such high expectations and not be able to see more progress toward reaching them. Personally, I think he expects too much since he stopped riding his bike even before he was diagnosed with Lewy body. And how many couch-potato-74-year-old-men are riding bikes even if they are well? Not many.

This afternoon, he sternly told me that I needed to get Mom to the doctor about pain that she's having in her legs. He is alarmed and knows what I should be telling her to do—the magnesium thing, still. Magnesium is curing cancer and Mom could have it in her bones. He needs to get the ball rolling by telling me to get on it. Never mind that Mom and I talk over her condition and options pretty much every morning. I've been helping her with all her medical decisions and know what she wants. I've also been doing the same for my aunt, oh, and for him, the husband, as well. But, it appears I am too slow now and need to be told what to do for her.

I was irritated and didn't give him the response he wanted. He is also irritated and grouchy. I know he feels like I don't take him seriously. It's true, I don't. But I kind of have to act like I do and then explain to him why I'm not hopping immediately to do his bidding. It's just confusing. This guy is so much like my husband, but he doesn't do any of the things a husband does. He doesn't plan. He doesn't make decisions. He doesn't think about things outside of his illness. He doesn't see me. I feel so selfish for caring about that. I am well. He is not. I wouldn't want to trade places with him either.

And since I can't take the steady dose of godly teaching from our "special station" and retreat to my room instead, I guess that makes me more toward the pagan end of the spectrum than he is. That also feels a bit uncomfortable, that and a lot of other things...

A Better Summer

June 6, 2020
Hayward, WI

April and May have come and gone. We are going cautiously into summer. I say cautiously because last summer is all too vivid in my memory. The plague of anxiety, the delusions, constant watchfulness and attempts to reassure, living in weird circumstances, trying to avoid electricity and evil spirits. Oh my. I am so glad we seem to have left that behind.

We have had a fall, winter, and spring of stable cognition and emotion. I am thankful. I cannot know for sure why it's been easier. I guess I don't need to know. We are continuing to do what we have been doing, in case some of that is helping. From time to time, Dennis thinks of adding or subtracting a supplement. If I don't think it makes a lot of difference, I don't argue about it, although I do get tired of the chore of filling the daily pill bottles.

Dennis elects to stay home more and more. He doesn't always go to visit relatives when I go, or out to eat either. With Covid-19 restrictions, he has gotten used to more inactivity—no church, no trips to the library or grocery store. TV is his entertainment, and I often find him with the TV on while he's also listening to something on his phone. But he is interested in what he watches and refers to a lot of it as his "research" on various topics.

He's done a lot of checking up on old friends from his days of teaching at Ambassador College.

He calls and follows the trail from one person to the next, finding out how they are. He sometimes picks up his horn and plays something. He tries to take one or two short walks every day or rides the stationary bike. He knows exercise is important, but he often is more comfortable sitting still.

His biggest problems are the constant tremor, in both hands now, overall weakness and instability, regulation of his bowel and bladder, some hypertensive spells, diminished sight and hearing, and the inability for planning or complex thinking. He does some of his own hygiene care, but I do have to shave him and remind him to shower and change clothes. He can get snacks from the fridge, but his meals are up to me most of the time. He's okay by himself at home, and I can leave him alone while I go to the garden or to Mom's for several hours at a time. All in all, life is still quite manageable and could be so much worse.

Curious things I notice:

It takes him a long time to come to his chair at the table, pull it out, position himself in front of it, and put his body down. Long time = almost forever.

His skin problems are still severe. He is always scratching skin flakes from his beard, neck, head.

His eyeglasses are always so dirty that I don't know how he sees through them. His shirts are always covered with skin flakes and are unsightly.

The shuffling is his normal walk now. He's started a forward lean that sometimes propels him forward faster than he wants to go. He looks old and frail when he walks, his hands shaking but not moving normally with his leg action.

His voice is hard to hear. He talks slowly, so slowly, and his words don't have edges that make them easy to distinguish. I'm always saying "what?"

He takes a morning nap and an afternoon nap most days.

So from day to day, not much has changed for the last few months, which is why it's hard to think what to write. We are mostly praying that he will be able to go to Seattle for a wedding in August (our youngest daughter) and another wedding in North Carolina sometime after that (our oldest daughter). Travel is not something he looks forward to anymore, so the planning will be challenging.

PART FIVE:
TWO PANDEMIC EVENTS

Covid Weddings

August 21, 2020
Hayward, WI

One thing that I have thought of fairly often since his diagnosis is that Dennis might not be around to witness some of the landmark events in his daughters' lives. I would never have imagined that both of our daughters would be contemplating marriage sometime in 2020, a year when the Covid pandemic was presenting challenges for any kind of gathering.

Youngest daughter, Esther, is newly engaged but is having problems getting a wedding venue out west in her state, where Covid is prevalent. Plans keep getting cancelled, and they are finally making the decision to wait until businesses open up again, probably in a year or so.

That is why we got very excited when Julia, the other daughter, and Kevin, her fiancé, decided to have their wedding this fall, in spite of the pandemic restrictions. Their venue is to be Kevin's farm, outdoors, with a limited number of guests. Party favors will be face masks in wedding colors that people can take home and use. It sounds doable.

October 10th has been chosen because it is a cool date (10/10/2020), will be easy to remember, and it is a Saturday. We have six weeks to prepare. I feel fairly certain that Dennis can make it to this one, and that will be a great relief. He's practicing what he wants to say when he gives his daughter away to the man she loves. It should be interesting.

I also like that this gives us something to think about and plan for other than Dennis's illness, a kind of shifting of our focus. I've got to dress the father of the bride, who has been wearing nothing but sweatpants, T-shirts, and moccasins for the last two years. Nothing else feels comfortable to him. I'm up for the challenge, but I'm thinking this job will not be simple or easy. There are no menswear stores in this town, and he's always been hard to fit. Not to mention, just try finding a pair of dress-up pants for a disabled man who doesn't do zippers, buttons, or belts.

Road Trip

September 28, 2020
Gibsonville, NC

We're in North Carolina for the wedding!

This week, the husband and I took a two-day drive to North Carolina for my daughter's wedding. Eighteen hours of driving have given me time to think about this process of road tripping, its advantages and disadvantages. See, it's really nice to have the freedom to go or stop at will. And there's the luxury of taking most anything I want along with me—in contrast to the "carry-on suitcase" limitations of flying. It's also nice to have that familiar vehicle at my destination without having to rent and return and get a big bill at the end.

BUT there are some slight disadvantages. For instance, I feel the full weight of staying awake and alert. I don't want to be like the guy who died peacefully in his sleep, unlike the screaming passengers in his car (an old joke we used to tell).

The husband is always chiding me for eating popcorn in the car without realizing that it has kept us alive for numerous trips. I can't sleep while I'm eating, or at least I haven't been able to so far. This trip, after I finished the popcorn, I started on the cheese curds, and then the nuts, and then the carrots/cucumbers/peppers. And then I felt ill, no surprise, but that also kept me awake.

Pandemic driving has some unique features, too. For once, we drove through the city of Chicago without a major slowdown. I was worried about going there, but having no good way to avoid it, we went. There was traffic, and the need for vigilance, but it was surprisingly smooth. And what's with the toll roads? There were no people in those little booths to collect money! I may have a massive bill lurking somewhere in cyberspace, but so far I've gotten no notice.

Then there is the mask thing. I can't remember how many times we were on our way into the rest stop or gas station and had to go back to get a required face covering. It's not a habit yet. We took food with us, not knowing if there would be the usual restaurants available. Finding a place to sit down and eat was harder, and the experience has changed in so many ways—no uncovered smiles, no condiments on the table, and not much merriment.

I knew it was a risk to get new tires right before a trip, but there were reasons why it made sense. I'm talking only hours before the trip, the dealership was able to find tires for my truck. There was no time to test them out. Did you know that pandemic shortages have affected the tire industry? Who would guess that? For this trip I went from worrying about old, misaligned, and worn tire noises to worrying about new tire noises. What is that whap, whap, whapping...? Is it lethal? Should we stop? We ignored it. Found out later that gravel and acorns caught in the tread sound just like defects. It made me wish for a man who knew about cars, tires, and things that go wrong on the road.

All in all, it was not a bad trip, just peculiar like most everything else in 2020 has been. Taking this trip, I found myself more content, perhaps even happy, with the thought of staying at home (like we're supposed to).

Wedding Prep

October 3, 2020
Gibsonville, NC

Preparing a wedding in six weeks seemed possible but a bit scary, given all that has come to be expected of weddings these days. And now, dresses have been chosen, decorations are being made, invitations are out, gifts are arriving. It is getting quite busy.

Dennis and I are staying at Julie's house, where I work on finishing touches for the wedding dress. It helps that we have stayed here before and Dennis is familiar with our surroundings.

Yesterday, after taste-testing the reception menu, I went out to work at the venue—the groom's farm and barn. I love to dig into dirt and dust where I can really see I've made a difference. There was an area of the barn that met this description, so I started dragging things out to be washed and de-spidered. Here's where a washing machine enters the story.

It was there to wash horsey things. It was dirty and heavy, but I wrangled it out on the lawn and sprayed it off with the hose. Later, I was wrestling it back in, inch by inch, back and forth. I distinctly remember the groom's eight-year-old daughter, who was helping, looking at me, watching intently, as I muscled the machine around for the last time. Her surprised face was the last thing I saw as my hand slipped on a backward pull. It was one of those moments when it's hard to believe what is happening, and you know you would like a "do-over." I fell on the concrete floor and the ensuing pain did not go away. I did break my fall, but I also broke my wrist.

So, instead of helping get things done during wedding week, I gave Julia new problems to deal with. She is an equine vet and hurried home from work with her mobile X-ray machine. The pictures confirmed that it was serious.

It's a good thing that Greensboro is a medically-oriented city, with an orthopedic urgent care clinic. I'm scheduled for surgery tomorrow with a nice, compassionate doctor. And maybe by Friday, I'll have a splint small enough to fit through the sleeve of my beautiful mother-of-the-bride dress.

All my life, I have never broken a bone anywhere in my body. Until now. Now, I need people to take care of me *and* my husband. It's kind of fitting, though, for a wedding in an already awkward pandemic year. It's one more thing to make it very memorable.

Giving Her Away

October 10, 2020
Gibsonville, NC

It's Saturday, the day of the wedding. At this point, there are so many details yet to be decided and attended to that it is a little frightening, but we have lots of help. It is raining lightly, and there are no alternate plans if the predicted bad weather comes. I have an unreasonable peace and trust that it will all come together, because the concerns have been given to God, and I know He means to give Julia a good wedding. I am going to get myself and the father of the bride dressed.

Two days later: I couldn't have imagined the changes that took place—all the beautiful flowers that arrived and the astounding transformation in the reception tent and the field where the ceremony was to be. Family and friends had pitched in to create a miracle. And the rain had let up, giving us a brief window of dryness.

Dennis wasn't able to walk in with the parents and the wedding party. He was already seated and waiting. However, he was ready for the question, "Who gives this woman in holy matrimony?"

"Her mother and I do, and don't give her back." Said with his quirky, mischievous smile.

As we watched the weather radar, the ceremony progressed. At one point, a song was omitted from the program to speed things along.

During the last five minutes, we began to feel an occasional raindrop. But it wasn't until we were dismissed and headed to the safety of the reception tent that the rain really began in earnest. By that time, we were so in awe of the beauty of the ceremony and the happiness of the bride and groom, and the timing of it all, that no one cared. Let it rain.

We feasted and danced as the North Carolina rain ran under the edges of the big white tent and met the red clay soil of River Bend Farm. It was wonderful. And the next day, I relived it all, as I spent a lot of time washing red mud out of the hem of a beautiful white dress.

One wedding down, one to go, and I'm hoping he makes it.

Twice Blessed

December 20, 2020
Hayward, WI

It just so happens that I have two men in this present stage of life who are near and dear to me. It just so happens that they are both named Dennis. It just so happens that they both have birthdays this week. Isn't that a little odd?

The one that I've known for the last 49 years is the husband Dennis. We are together, still, and figuring out life together, one day at a time. He will be 75 on Friday, not that he takes much stock in birthdays, his or anyone else's.

The second Dennis is my brother. I've known him for all of his life. He came on the scene when I was ten years old, the youngest of my four brothers. His birthday is tomorrow, Monday. He might as well have been born on Christmas, since the holiday lasts nearly a week for all practical purposes. It's easy to get overlooked in a very busy season.

That's why I'm sitting here feeling twice blessed for having two cherished relationships in a world where many people don't have that. It's a good ending to a very unusual year.

Kinesiology

January 5, 2021
Hayward, WI

Today we went to a chiropractor who has been doing applied kinesiology for Dennis. The functional medicine doctor recommended this kind of therapy, hoping to get some information that might have been missed before. Dennis hasn't been able to get rid of his tremor, in both hands now, or regain strength with all of the treatments he's been on. Doctor Nan is rather desperately looking for something else.

Dennis likes the chiropractor. In one session, he tested weak in an area and the practitioner asked if he had unresolved issues of shame in his childhood. It progressed into a surprising memory that surfaced and an emotional discussion that we all thought was beneficial. Today, the doctor told me he felt there was still something more, but it would have to wait until he could schedule a longer session with Dennis.

This search for reversal of his dementia is really calling on every bit of patience I can muster. There are so many things I have to do for Dennis to get him ready to go anywhere. He needs help with almost all his hygiene tasks, starting with being reminded that he needs to do them. His fingernails would be two inches long if I didn't tell him they needed to be clipped—except for the right hand. He chews them off on that side.

Everything he is able to do himself is done at turtle speed because his mind is trying to remember the steps. I am realizing how complex many of our movements are and how we take them for granted. What is automatic for everyone else is not for Dennis. For instance, the chiropractor has a very narrow adjusting table. Dennis has to lie down on it, and he is clueless about how to do it except if he is helped. But turning over onto his stomach without falling off the table is almost impossible. It took more than five minutes just to figure out a strategy, let alone execute it, even with the chiropractor and me helping.

Light therapy, sound frequency therapy, essential oil therapy, as well as all the regular chiropractic adjusting, get done every time we go there. We also have potions from a company called CellCore for mitochondrial support and ATP function, Hydroxygen for energy and detox support, a mineral supplement, and a parasitical. Evidently, there are parasites present somewhere. After one appointment, Dennis came home with acupuncture needles still embedded in his scalp and ears for me to remove. But I really haven't seen any positive changes over the last month. I know these things take time, but even the chiropractor thought there would be some improvement by now.

Dennis also thought there would be improvement by now. I know he is getting impatient and wants to do something more, but he is not as good at researching anymore. He has trouble reading anything, his hearing is problematic (as are the hearing aids), and he falls asleep easily. I fear that maybe I should be taking up the search. I have my doubts that he is capable of carrying out the kind of program that would bring reversal, if it is even possible.

I admit it. I'm having trouble taking care of both of us. I fantasize about having time to shower and cut MY fingernails, fix MY hair. I would like to figure out how I'm supposed to be eating, and why my blood pressure is going up. It would be so nice to go out to dinner or have coffee with a friend somewhere outside the house. But I suppose someday that will be possible, even though the road could be long. LBD has a prognosis of death within an average of 5-8 years, but some people live much longer. I think about that a lot. I wonder how Dennis feels about it, but I don't ask.

He Stayed Alone

April 22, 2021
Hayward, WI

It's been two and a half years since diagnosis, and changes are still gradual. Most of them have been physical and are movement disorders. The shuffling, the tremor that started in the right hand and now affects both, sometimes a tremor in the legs, incredible slowness of movement, and a blank facial expression—all those symptoms have been the most noticeable. Even with these things, Dennis has still been mostly independent. He moves himself from one place to the other, gets to the bathroom without help, puts himself to bed, gets a snack when he wants one, and makes decisions to go to church or the chiropractor or to visit Mom or my brother.

Cognitively, he is able to think and remember fairly well. He brightens up when talking with friends on the phone and carries on a meaningful conversation, although slowly. Sometimes he snaps into his scientific mind and amazes people. He has become focused on a few subjects, which he follows by listening to YouTube podcasts on his phone. He has a list of prophets that provide daily updates, and he often listens to the same one several times a day. I think he really wishes Jesus would come again and put an end to his misery.

He doesn't spend as much time researching his own disease, although he runs across something every now and then. He is more centered on the supernatural, hoping for a better chance with God than he has noticed with medicine. The most recent therapy that he is still receiving is applied kinesiology, which includes chiropractic, muscle testing, light therapy, nerve stimulation, craniosacral therapy, and tapping, all from the same practitioner, who also prays with him.

He was alone at home for one week in April while I took Mom to Florida for a memorial and family visit. He had my brother and Lurae, a neighbor, looking in on him and providing meals. He seemed to be fine with that. My brother remarked that he perhaps did things better than he does when he's being waited on all the time. Interesting.

But I think I notice, following that week, a tendency to sleep more during the day, and not as well at night. It looks a lot like depression, and why would it not? There is so little he feels he can do except listen to his phone. That gets tiring, so he goes and takes a nap.

Last night, he could not tell what the food on his plate was. He was trying to cut it up as if it were chicken, but to his surprise, it was salmon. He had a lot of trouble getting food on his fork and reverted to using his fingers to eat the fish and green beans, which is okay with me, but messy. He took a spoonful of cranberry relish and thought he was putting it on his plate, but no, he was purposely putting it on a napkin that he thought was his plate. I think the whole mealtime experience devastated him.

When I asked if he was having more trouble with his eyes, he said yes, and that he thought it was probably his brain rather than his macular degeneration getting worse. He was very resigned and quiet about it.

As always, I question whether we are heading into a period of more noticeable changes? I hope he will still be able to travel to our Esther's wedding in July. He was so looking forward to that.

Good Advice

April 25, 2021
Hayward, WI

I frequently read posts in a caregiver group for Lewy body dementia. Tonight, I was glad for the advice I commonly see there concerning changes in behavior. The advice is to always suspect a urinary tract infection.

The last two or three days have been bad ones for Dennis. He has been weaker, sleeping more, hard to motivate, less interactive, not eating as well, not thinking as well. He needed a shower (smelled bad), and although he didn't object to the idea, he would never get around to doing it. He would take a nap instead.

He began having urinary incontinence problems and wanted to know where his Depends were. He would wake up with an urgent need for the bathroom, but would have so much difficulty getting there that he would have an accident. Finally, he told me he had a burning sensation when he started to urinate, and the light in my brain came on. UTI.

Why do these things always happen on the weekend? Fortunately, we do have an urgent care clinic at our hospital, and I decided to take him there right away. He had to be talked into going—"I've had these kinds of problems for months," he said. But I told him we needed to find out, and that it would be fairly simple to do, and that it would not be good to wait for an appointment during the week.

We were in an exam room within a few minutes after checking in. Vital signs showed normal blood pressure and temperature, so no fever. A urine sample was taken, as well as an ultrasound of the bladder to see if there was more than usual residual. The results showed a lot of white cells (infection) and some blood in the urine as well. Before we went home, he was given an injection, a prescription for 10 days of oral antibiotics, and orders to check back in a couple of days.

I am so glad we are on to this! It could explain all the recent changes that have worried me. Hopefully, the infection clears up and we won't have to deal with worse complications like kidney stones or kidney infection.

I thank God for His promptings, for bringing things to mind, and for the appropriate sense of urgency to get care quickly. We ask for His help daily, and He is good to us.

A Bad, Scary Day

May 29, 2021
Hayward, WI

A strange occurrence this week. The husband had a bad day, which was noticed first when we went a few doors over to my brother's house for a meal. He had a very hard time seeing things, like steps to go up or down, and food on his plate. He was very quiet at the meal but still conversed. Being very tired afterwards, he went for a nap.

When he woke up, he was confused and couldn't verbalize well. Words would come out of his mouth that he had no idea he had spoken, words that didn't mean what he intended to say. He didn't know why. All evening, he looked at me strangely, his eyes full of questions and alarm. He acknowledged that something was very different and very wrong. He was slower in his movements, but was able to get around okay, and seemed weak but symmetrical in his muscle tone.

His blood pressure was very high, something that had become common for him. His usual methods of bringing it down were not as effective, but as the evening wore on it did come down. LBD is known for erratic spikes in blood pressure in spite of medication. I wondered if he had experienced a small stroke.

The next day he was not as scary in his reactions but still very bothered by his inability to think and verbalize. He concluded that some damage had been done and it could take a while for him to recover.

Another change has been his willingness to accept a wheelchair. He has needed one the last couple of times at the doctor's office. He can't stand in lines to wait, and has felt generally much weaker and in need of sitting. He has stopped doing exercise except on rare occasions. He can't walk very far and wants to have the walker in the car whenever we go somewhere. His overall appearance is of a very disabled man.

There are ups and downs, relapses and recoveries with LBD, but I would have to say that he has clearly progressed in the disease. He has not been making phone calls since having the speech trouble, and that is sad, because it was a lifeline for him. I'm hoping that he will improve in that area.

That Strange Thing

May 31, 2021
Hayward, WI

I don't think he had a stroke. I think it was one of the expected fluctuations of LBD.

For a day, he had difficulty thinking fast enough to speak and getting words out, but now he apparently has recovered. Last night, he held a phone conversation without trouble, and today he enjoyed a long talk with a new friend. I could see no effect from his temporary lapses.

I also asked him if he felt recovered, and he thinks yes, he has. He's physically slow but mentally back to par (for him).

Just like his blood pressure has dramatic spikes, followed by strange lows, the other parts of his nervous system experience blips in their function. Sometimes it's his eyesight, sometimes bowel function, often it's coordinating his movements. Again, it's life on the roller coaster of LBD. We just don't know what to expect next.

I think it does help to pray and have a positive attitude. I'm grateful it does not seem to be the "fall from the cliff" that I thought it might be.

Get This Off My Phone

June 5, 2021
Hayward, WI

Today, the husband came to me in my "girl cave" wanting to know if I could fix something on his phone. He had inadvertently taken a video of his knee and posted it on Facebook. A fairly complicated accident, if you ask me.

There were already two comments on it from friends, which was nice, but he hadn't seen them yet. Instead he was frustrated over an email ad offering to take down an unwanted photo from an unnamed site.

Is there some internet business just scrolling Facebook, finding weird videos, and marketing themselves as being able to solve some horrible problem? I don't know. I just edited the Facebook post. I could have deleted it, but the friend messages were nice and I thought he should keep them. The episode made me wonder if he could get into trouble with the things he does on his phone...

It is his dearest occupation—to watch/listen to podcasts and videos on his phone. It's close, in his hand, and the screen is magnified to a size he can read. It talks to him and gives him things to think about. I don't know what could replace it in his limited arsenal of things to do.

His inability to see things for what they are, such as advertisements, is constantly coming up in our conversations. He is very swayed by clever marketing and feels like he has "discovered" things by his "research."

Lately he has been "researching" a problem my mom has been having and is certain he can help her with it. Last night, when I had disappeared on a bike ride, he went over to Mom's, uninvited, and was sitting talking with her when I stopped in. When I left them to get a shower and go to bed, he didn't want to come home with me. He sat and talked until nearly 10 pm.

I wasn't sure if I should make him come with me, but I figured Mom could handle it if she wanted him to leave. She said he told a lot of old stories (no surprise there). Her comment was, "he doesn't get bored when he's doing the talking." Not always the case with those who are listening.

He didn't remember to tell her about his research and wanted to try again today. He loves my mom.

It's sad. Sometimes it's frustrating. But he is still interested in life. He's kind, cooperative, funny, and really not that much more work than I'm used to anyway. And I have so many places to find joy that it amazes me. God is good, even (especially) in this phase of our lives.

We are okay, at least until I can no longer figure out technology either...

A New Chair

June 24, 2021
Hayward, WI

Dennis has been getting more receptive to equipment that makes movement easier for him, like the wheelchair. He always used to say no to those things, thinking that he should continue to do everything the hard way, under his own steam, because it was "exercise." But now his slowness and instability make it hard for me to take him places, even close places like Mom's house, or to my brother's, which is an easy walking distance (for anyone but Dennis).

So the first concession was to start using a walker. We had a low-end model but he found it hard to go over uneven sidewalks because the walker had only two wheels, and the other contact with the ground was just aluminum legs, which often got hung up. I guess that's why people buy tennis balls and stick them on the legs.

Then he discovered Mom's fancy convertible wheelchair, which can be used as a walker and also has a seat. It is extra security when he gets tired and needs to rest. He hardly ever goes far enough to need to rest, but that is beside the point. The seat is there and ready.

Yesterday, he broke down and said he needed a lift chair. We had been noticing the increased struggle getting out of recliners. He loves to spend most of his time in that type of chair, but it would take him a half-dozen attempts to get out of one. He has very little strength in his thighs. At the same time, he had been having frequent urges to get to the bathroom, which was not good when he was stuck in his chair. He had tried Mom's lift chair last week and found it quite impressive. He wanted one.

There are two furniture stores in Hayward—the expensive one and the less expensive but still horrifying one. In the lesser store, I found two chairs, both of which were just a bit under $2,000. They also looked huge, and I am not a fan of huge, heavy furniture anymore.

I didn't even bother with the expensive store. Instead, I went to Facebook Marketplace and inquired about three that were within reasonable driving distance.

This morning, I borrowed my brother's truck, picked up a strong helper, drove an hour away to Ashland, and fetched home a chair. The upholstery is in great shape, and it only cost a quarter of what a new one would cost. I could be happier about the electronics, which are a bit confusing, but it does a nice powered recline and it does eject him satisfactorily. There was no place to plug it in for a test at the storage facility where we picked it up.

I don't know, it seems really big to me...

I think he's happy tonight. He likes it (thankfully). I think it's a comfortable chair, although I've only sat in it once. It's quite a piece of furniture, with a "presence" all its own. I'm afraid it might even have a personality. I can imagine it getting mad at him, rising up, and dumping him on the floor. And what's with all the unused cords that are taped on the underside? If ever a chair could dominate a room, it would be this one. It might need a name. At the very least, it calls for a living room re-arrange, since it looks really weird in its high, tilted position, waiting for its occupant. I'm hoping to dream up the new arrangement while I sleep tonight. I'll find a good place for it. Welcome, Mr. Chair.

Traveling Again

July 22, 2021
Seattle, WA

Our daughter, Esther, loves living in the Pacific Northwest even though we wish she weren't two time zones away. She has been planning to get married for nearly two years. Covid problems caused two cancellations, but the date was rescheduled for this coming Saturday. We were not going to let Lewy body keep us from being here, and it hasn't. We are here. As far as we know, it is going to happen in two days.

I planned this trip for months in order to get comfortably from Wisconsin to Seattle, Washington. We could have flown, but I think Dennis was afraid of that kind of experience. Instead, he wanted a road trip over the northern states that he used to travel frequently for business. I thought it might be a good thing for him to relive those memories.

The trip took five days of travel and four nights in motels, which I reserved ahead. I didn't know how tired he would get riding, so kept most of the days at about six hours on the road, with stops as needed to stretch. I'm not saying it was easy, but we did it.

His movement problems and weakness have increased over the last month or two, and sitting for hours in the car seemed to tire him more than sitting in his recliner at home. I found out that his frequent naps at home were what he was missing—being horizontal for an hour or two was what he needed. At the end of our travel days, he was ready to sit in the wheelchair and be taken into the hotel. He would lie down immediately and sleep.

I know I repeat this a lot, but I marvel at how slowly he moves. I'm always thinking that it couldn't get any worse, but then it does. It's not so bad when I'm the only one waiting on him, but often he's standing in a doorway trying to figure out how and where to walk, with a line of people behind him waiting to get in. People are kind and say it's okay, but nevertheless, it is hard to be the ones causing the roadblocks.

Getting up out of chairs is a terrible ordeal, and walking up or down steps is even harder. His legs tremble and he looks like he could fall at any moment. He uses a walker and a cane in places where the wheelchair will not go. His fear of falling is part of what makes him so slow and cautious, but he also has difficulty remembering how to move his body.

Movements that used to be automatic now take conscious, slow effort. In motels, beds that are higher are hard to get into, and once in them he can't straighten or position his body so he sleeps diagonally, in whatever position he lands.

It really amazes me that he is able to get himself up at night to the bathroom in motel rooms that are unfamiliar without falling or hurting himself. I dread the day when he cannot do it anymore.

Travel has messed with his eyesight, too, or maybe I notice it more because I am with him all day and we are looking at the scenery going by. He is frequently asking what something is that he thinks he sees, and then I have to try to guess what he's looking at so I can tell him what it really is. His depth perception is terrible (or almost absent). He can't tell whether an object appears big because it is close, or because it is actually big and far away. His inability to gauge step height is so bad that he uses his cane to "feel" it. He looks like a blind man walking. He needs to be led to the men's restroom, and I'm afraid to know what goes on inside when I can't go in with him.

And speaking of restrooms, there is another topic that has given us some adventures. Urinary frequency and incontinence are problems in themselves, even more so when one moves with the speed of a sloth.

Whenever there is a one-person restroom, I go in with Dennis and help him because his dexterity and eyesight are problems—he often comes out with wetness on his pants, fly open, drawstrings dangling from his waist.

Sometimes he sits and the toilet is so low that he has trouble getting up again and needs to be helped up. Sometimes the pad he wears in his pants needs to be changed, and sometimes I tell him to just go in his pants because the pad will catch it easier than us trying to get to the bathroom. He resists that, and I can understand, but hey... you gotta go.

Food is getting to be a problem, too. There are quite a few things that he just doesn't like to order because they have to be cut or chewed. It's too much work. It's hard for him to focus on a written menu, so I usually read it to him and suggest things. He eats with his fingers a lot of the time because he knows he can get it into his mouth that way. Aiming a fork at lettuce and hoping for the best doesn't work well. Things fall off his fork and spoon and land on his shirt or the floor, and that bothers him a lot.

West Coast Wedding Week

July 23, 2021
Seattle, WA

For the last few days, we have been in our hotel in Seattle with Julia and Kevin and the three stepchildren who all flew in from North Carolina. We are car sharing so they won't have to get a rental. They want to give the children a chance to see some West Coast sites. I'm not sure the kids are enjoying themselves. They have numerous complaints, starting with the five of them being cooped up in one hotel room. I've had these step-grandchildren less than a year and am not quite used to them yet.

Dennis has stayed back at the hotel for a lot of our meals out. Luckily, he has a Keurig and a cooler in the hotel room. It's tremendously confusing trying to find a place everyone wants to eat, a place that can seat all of us, and if Dennis does go, a place he can get into without us having to carry him in. It's a lot of work.

We have made several nice excursions. One was to Vashon Island to see a house that Esther and her fiancé had purchased. Another was to what would have been the rehearsal dinner, had there been a rehearsal. This dinner was held on a beautiful night at Salty's on the waterfront with a view of the city and all its lights. It's been so nice to have people who help us get parked in these unfamiliar places. Dennis got seated where he could see people and talk easily. He stayed in one place the whole time. I think he had fun.

I can tell when he is getting tired and is trying to pace himself here at wedding week. But he is pretty happy at seeing both of his daughters and so many other family members. We have quite a crowd here.

He Was There

July 24, 2021
Seattle, WA

What a beautiful day it has been. The wedding was at the Arboretum, and since it was outside there wasn't a lot of concern about masking. We came a little early, and I helped with some last-minute decorations.

Esther had her Airstream trailer on site as her dressing area, which was only one of the unique features of this wedding. She had chosen a poem for me to read as part of the ceremony, but it was pretty evident that Dennis was not going to be comfortable with any of the usual "dad" duties. He did get a seat at a table in the front with a great view of it all.

After the bride and groom entered, Esther came over to Dennis where he was seated and gave him the best hug and a kiss. He stayed seated and didn't say anything, but he felt acknowledged. He was moved, and there were tears.

The reception was a pizza bar, and pie was also the "new wedding cake." Dennis had a few conversations but was silently watching most of the time. There was dancing afterwards as the evening deepened, and I know the family had a memorable time because the pictures and videos we saw later were sweet. We, however, left early, which felt good because it had been a long day.

He was there, and that was what mattered. Mission accomplished.

The Trip Home

July 30,2021
Hayward, WI

Our trip out had taken five days, but I decided we needed to get back in less time, so we went quickly to the larger interstate highways. We had some nice stops, though. One stop in Alberton, MT was at a small motel right on a large river. It was so close to a steep bank at the river's edge that Dennis was worried he might accidentally go out the back door of our room and fall in. Fortunately, the room was so small that the bed blocked the door. I was able to convince him not to worry.

Interstate travel is good in that the rest stops are frequent enough and have handicapped facilities. But they are also boring and seemingly endless through North Dakota and Minnesota. Because of fires in Canada, there was a lot of smoke in the air. During the longer hours of driving, Dennis didn't say much, and I didn't realize how difficult they were for him until the end of the third day. We were getting out of the car, and he almost collapsed before I could get the wheelchair under him. I'm not sure what I would have done if he had fallen.

We were home in the late afternoon of the fourth day, and I helped him to bed for a nap. It's so good to be back where the risk factor is not so great. I can hardly believe that we did this.

Telephone Tribe

August 13, 2021
Hayward, WI

I've just read something in an online support group for dementia caretakers that made me think. It was about how those with a diagnosis of LBD who have been good friends with many in better years don't hear from their friends anymore. Actually, it was a caretaker writing the post, who was sad that the friends didn't even contact her to ask how her husband was. She was wondering what their excuses were. Were they unable to handle the changes they saw in him? Were they afraid dementia was contagious, or that they would somehow get it? Did they think that their absence wouldn't be noticed by anyone, so why bother?

My husband, who has Lewy body dementia, is probably not your typical dementia victim because he has refused to let people forget him. He calls them up if he knows their number. He hunts them down if he doesn't know their number. He calls them again if they don't answer the first, second, or third time he calls. He checks up on them even if they don't check up on him. He remembers what they've talked about. These people are his past business associates, the members of the band he used to play in, and family members.

Many times I've listened to the conversations (he is always in the living room and doesn't try to keep them private). Sometimes I cringe when I hear him repeating the same story to someone who has heard it all before. Sometimes I feel sorry for the person he calls because he talks so slowly and often has trouble hearing.

Sometimes I wish he wouldn't try to sound like an authority about other people's problems, or misquote things he's read, or be so simplistic about things I think are much more complex. But at the end of it all, I see that there are those people who do take his calls anyway. There are some who listen to his stories, even if somewhat impatiently, and respond with interest. Some tell him that he has encouraged them, given them hope. They are his telephone tribe.

I hear patience in their voices when they talk to him, laugh with him, ask him questions. When they don't have time for his hour-long versions, they tell him they need to go in a few minutes. They set limits in kind ways and show respect. They call him back when they say they will or apologize if they forget. They continue to be good friends. They know they are doing something for him that friendship is supposed to do, and they are not afraid, not too busy, not "turned off" by the changes dementia has brought to him.

I am so thankful for those friends, because they also help me. I am thankful to have married a man who chose his friends wisely.

What Hope Can Do

August 21, 2021
Hayward, WI

I haven't recorded all the things that Dennis has gotten through lately, and since they are remarkable they should be recorded.

We're in a stage where the doctors seem to be done with him. No one is checking him or recommending new treatments. He has discontinued some of the supplements that didn't seem to have much effect but were costing a lot of money. It could be viewed as a discouraging time, but he remains outwardly hopeful and unperturbed.

Yesterday morning, praying about the day ahead, God and I came to an agreement. Our new son-in-law's parents were coming from Seattle for their first visit to our area, and I had arranged with a friend for a boat ride on our favorite lake. I knew it would be kind of weird for Dennis not to be there with us, but I questioned whether we could get him in the boat easily. Even he had said he would just stay home because it sounded hard. We had done this same excursion two years ago with different friends, and it had been hard then. He has declined a lot since.

Back to the agreement. I felt that I should ask Dennis again if he wanted to go on the boat, and if he did, we would plan on it and God would help us. As I suspected, Dennis wanted to go. Here's how it went down.

We arrived at "Lunch on the Lake" and talked with Mr. Jacobsen, the boat captain. He allowed us to drive down the steep embankment on their lawn to get near their boat dock. Dennis used his walker to finish the distance and get out on the long, narrow dock. It took a great deal of coaching and encouragement from all five of us to tell him where to hang on, which part of him to move next, how high to lift his feet, when to duck under the boat awning, etc, and we were ready to catch him at any moment if we had to, but he made it. It was remarkable because this is a guy who often has trouble just getting in bed.

We had a good hour-long boat ride and a nice lunch with our guests before we had to repeat the whole process in reverse. I think we all had a sense of accomplishment when it was over and we were in the car again. We did a little more sightseeing with him riding in the wheelchair, and by the time company left, he was ready for his overdue nap.

But I can see what hope can do! Sometimes God gives us challenges and wants to see what we will do with them. With the challenge, He promises to help, to teach, to show up in some way to demonstrate remarkable things. I am so thankful we are not on this journey alone.

Being Right

August 29, 2021
Hayward, WI

(It has been suggested by the husband that I write this to our daughters. He wants them to know he loves them.)

We were reading a thoughtful paragraph on humility this morning, referencing people who always think they are right about anything and everything. Dennis laughed and said something that our youngest daughter had said to him once. "I am right, because I am a Dietz!" It was said jokingly, tongue in cheek, and they laughed at it at the time, too. Then he got quiet and continued, "I love our daughters so much. I hope they know that."

I loved hearing him say that. It was a special moment, and we continued talking about the meaning of that conversation and why the memory of it sparked such gratitude and love inside his "dad heart."

During the years our daughters were growing up at home, there were so many good times for us as parents and for them as children. There were also times, not so good, when they felt distanced from their parents. The role of provider was always of great concern for Dennis and required a lot of his attention. Maybe small people (his children), having limited experiences, were not as interesting as other friends and business associates. He never intentionally conveyed this to them, but it was conveyed nonetheless.

In addition, it was natural to assume that children's opinions, reasons, and thought processes were still to be directed and molded, not listened to and considered. This attitude also was never intentionally spoken, nor was it applied 100% of the time, but over the years it was felt, sometimes acutely. Although Dad provided well and loved them, he didn't know them personally and was often clueless as to what they were feeling. Perhaps they heard more of "don't leave toothpaste in the sink" and "your lights were left on—go turn them off" than the things daughters need to hear from their dads.

So what does it mean when a daughter can tease, laugh, and point out some hurtful flaw when talking to her dad? What did it mean that she could remind him of his "always right" attitude in a gentle conversation? To him, it meant forgiveness. It meant that she wasn't afraid to remind him of that proclivity of his. It was acknowledgement and grace extended. And it was love.

The husband has mellowed so much in the last few years. Retirement has put the distraction of being a provider behind him. He fully realizes those things he has missed by not being more aware, more curious, more persistent about knowing his children. He has also been diagnosed with a heartbreaking condition. But it has turned into a blessing. It's almost as if his heart had to be broken in order for him to know what was in it. It's amazing to think about.

Although he is disabled, he has traveled long distances to see each of his two daughters get married during pandemic times. He would not have missed these opportunities for the world. "Being right" has come full circle and is now much more like "Being in love."

It provides hope for us all. We can grow, learn, and change. The whole story doesn't have to be pretty for the outcome to be good. God be praised for His transforming power, His gentleness, His wisdom, and His mysterious ways.

Another Long Winter

December 9, 2021
Hayward, WI

It is a stunning realization—we have begun our fourth winter since the husband's diagnosis of LBD. It is hard to say if the things we have done since September 2018 have been the right things, or have been done consistently or for long enough time. It's just hard to imagine that one could quickly change the course of a disease that's been in progress for many years. We may not have stopped it in its tracks, but it is clear that our journey is different from that of most others, so far.

LBD quickly becomes a story told by the caregiver. I remember attending a conference for LBD patients and their spouses/caretakers at Mayo Clinic in 2019 where a patient was one of the main speakers. He did a good job. I wonder how he is now. I have a feeling he was a rare case.

My Dennis used to think and talk about the book he was going to write telling his experience with LBD, and his reversal of the disease, of course. That doesn't get mentioned anymore. He doesn't write anything, and sometimes has trouble signing his name. A book is not the kind of project he would have been motivated to finish even when he was well, so it is not surprising to me that it has never even been started. Talking has always been his mode of communication. LBD has not changed that.

He has cognitive deficits that he is aware of, but his personality is intact. His curiosity and desire to learn are still there. His need to teach and share what he knows is still prevalent. He surprised us all over the Thanksgiving holiday by having some fairly deep conversations with several people, in which he almost seemed normal in a "pre-Lewy" way. He listens every morning when we read. He asks intelligent questions and makes reasonable comments. But prolonged thinking tires him out, and he no longer tries to convince, debate, or argue his points.

I left this morning to take Mom to an early doctor appointment. Dennis was listening to a favorite podcast and started to tell me something he thought was very important, which I didn't have time to hear. When I asked him at lunch what the important thing was, he couldn't remember it. He said he was having more trouble with his memory again. It did finally come to him, but he had to ask me to find the podcast for him on his phone and play it over.

I've been gone most of the day, taking Mom to appointments and for groceries. He sits in his lift chair, silence in the room—a rare occasion. I ask him what's on his mind and if he needs socialization from me. He says "no." He's thinking about a sermon he heard earlier on TV. I don't believe him. I sit down and tell him about my day and read to him.

Memory Exercise

December 17, 2021
Hayward, WI

In our married years, the husband and I and the girls have spent considerably more time with my family than with his. I was always the one who took the kids on vacation, and it was easier to go to a place I was familiar with. I always knew that I would be able to fit in, help out, and not have to be entertained by my folks. By our sixth year of marriage, both of Dennis's parents had died, so that made it harder to visit Pennsylvania, too. His brother and sister both had young, active families. They were busy.

For some reason, a few days ago, I began thinking about how I would go about helping my girls know this half of their heritage. I wasn't clear on some of the stories (of which there are many) told at their family gatherings, and I couldn't even remember the names of all the husband's aunts and uncles. Clearly, I needed to do something about this void of information, especially since I have the husband available to me, and he loves to remember. The girls also love that side of the family, even though they don't know them quite as well.

So this week, after our Bible reading time, I have been asking Dennis questions about the family for an hour or two. It doesn't take much to get him going. Since he talks kind of slowly, I can keep up with him, typing out what he says. It was often said of him that he had a photographic memory and amazing recall of things said, as well as things seen. It has perhaps grown a little "fuzzy" with his dementia problems, but if he hits a wall on something, he calls his brother Ron and they talk it out.

It's been interesting, and what a worthy project. I have learned so much about interviewing. Many things I would not have thought about asking Dennis for my own sake, I do think of asking for my girls—things kids want to know about their parents. These are stories and facts that they should know in order to value the general concept of family as well as their own particular family.

And as an added bonus, this might be just what I need right now to help me appreciate what an interesting person I have been married to these last 49 years.

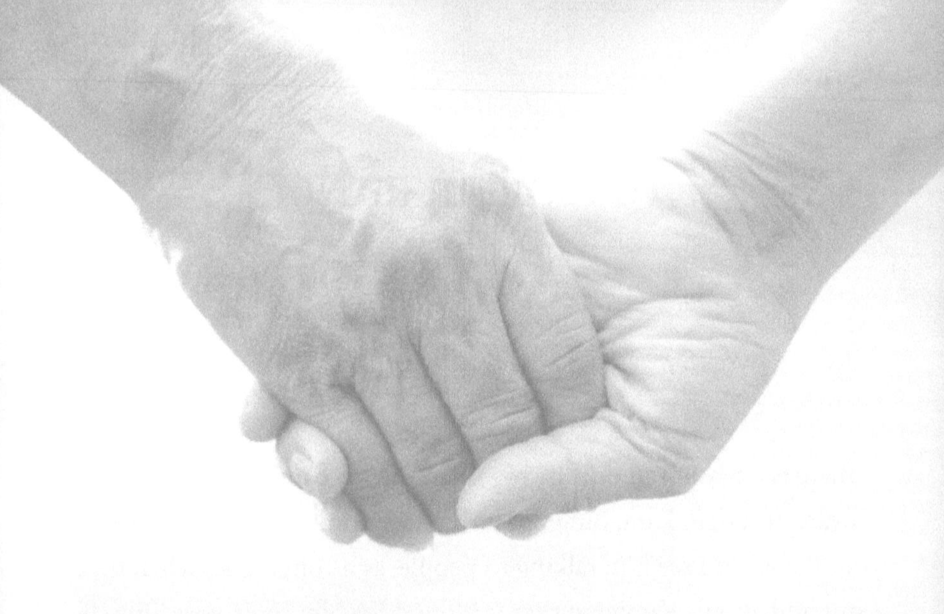

PART SIX: THEN EVERYTHING CHANGED

To Explain or Not

January 28, 2022
Hayward

There is a tension in our life together, the husband and I. He is less aware of it than I am, but even he feels it at times. The tension arises for me when I see him talking to people, as he often does when he's out and about. Knowing that it is good for him to express himself and socialize, I usually just watch. But I also know that eventually I will have to decide whether or not to step in and rescue.

Rescue who? Usually, it's the kind person who has decided to engage him in conversation.

Before Dennis had the diagnosis of Lewy body dementia, I didn't feel responsible for rescuing anyone, well, hardly ever. Before Lewy, he would often get in his "teacher" mode and give long lectures, complete with multiple rabbit trails. Since I had heard it all before, I would let him and his audience fend for themselves. His topics were still reasonably interesting to a lot of people hearing them for the first time. Others knew not to get him started.

But now, I have his reputation and his dignity to defend. His topics are much narrower and not always interesting to others. He's not good at reading body language and knowing that he's losing his listener's attention. Sometimes his discretion is not in play and he says things he shouldn't. We talk when we're alone about these times, and he is thoughtful and serious about doing better.

Other times, he listens as well as he can to conversations, but doesn't hear or understand important parts of them. I'm often surprised to find out what he thinks he has heard. He still cares about his interactions with people. He often wants to go over and talk with Mom. He loves to go to church activities. He listens to his favorite people on YouTube and other social media so regularly that they seem like family. His personality is still intact and recognizable. He is still himself, and what a good thing that is! I'm more than thankful.

The fact remains. I spend quite a bit of time explaining Dennis and his intentions to others, and a lot of time explaining others to him. I feel like the gateway to his awareness of the world, and somehow that bothers me.

The Last Voluntary Trip

April 17, 2022
North Carolina

We have let enough time pass since the last trip for the memories to fade and not be quite so awful. I knew the time would come when we would have to try another trip, and that time has come. We have unfinished business in North Carolina, in our daughter's basement, which is partly our reason for going. The other part is that we need to see them more often and want to do our part by going to them. We may not always be able to do that.

Preparing for travel is my first job. I have mapped my route and made hotel reservations for two nights on the road. Both nights find us in towns where I have relatives, and in another life, I might have asked to stay with them, but not now. I am so glad that we can afford to choose lodging that suits Dennis's needs and gives us a chance to get a good night's sleep.

Our second night is in Madison, Indiana where my cousin and her husband have been developers, overseeing the remodeling of an old, abandoned cotton mill into a Fairfield Inn. It was a big project, and has added a valuable historic site to the city's list of places to visit. We are actually going to be staying there, as well as having dinner with Ron and Marlene. This will be our biggest "treat" of the three days of travel.

Later: Our trip proceeded pretty much as planned. The unexpected difficulties were Dennis's persistent, recurring nosebleeds and a bout of stomach upset that kept him from taking his meds for a few days. He decided he was doing well without the meds and wouldn't start taking them again—just his supplements. I didn't argue with him because I couldn't tell if he was worse in any way either.

We accomplished our mission in North Carolina. Painfully, I went through every box and evaluated every stored thing from our past Florida life. I sold one piece of furniture before Julie convinced me that she wanted the rest for a garage sale she intends to have. I spent quite a few hours sorting and pulling out a few small things that would come back to Wisconsin in the car with us. We had a very full load.

Dennis tried hard not to be too needy. He sat in the bedroom watching TV and his phone for most of the two weeks. We did spend some good times with Kevin, Julia, and the three children. I think Dennis enjoyed that. They gave up their master bedroom and bath for us, and it was quite adequate, although any change takes getting used to when you have disabilities.

We traveled back in two days. We always seem to be motivated to spend longer hours in the car on the way home. Our last day, driving up through Wisconsin, was rainy and then snowing. Welcome home. I've said it before, but maybe this really will be the last time we travel together.

May Update

May 5, 2022
Hayward, WI

Yesterday's thought-provoking incident happened around supper time for us. The family had scheduled a Zoom conference to do some advance planning for our summer reunion. I came over to the husband, who was sitting in his lift chair with the TV on, his eyes closed. I told him I was going over to Mom's house to help her get on Zoom. She is always confused about computer events.

He opened his eyes and listened to me, but had such a blank expression that I started over and reminded him of the details, the Zoom, of the reunion we were planning, and watched him get totally confused by it all. He said so, repeatedly. "I'm confused. I don't know, I'm just confused." He couldn't find more words to describe his mental state, and that alone was causing him concern. I could see that he was getting frightened.

"Can we pray about it?" he finally asked, shaking his head. So we did.

He then decided that the best thing would be to go back to his bed, even though he had only been up for about half an hour from his last nap. I watched him closely as he went to the bathroom, took off his glasses and hearing aids and lay down. He was a bit confused even in that routine. But he slept for a couple hours, got up and ate supper, and apparently felt more himself.

What was going on there? I don't know. But I realized that I was past the point of rushing him to the ER for stroke intervention or any other kind of help. He didn't ask to go either. Weird changes have become so normal. Some of them I've just read about and others have actually happened to us. Once, he told me he couldn't see the food on his plate and wondered what was happening to his eyes. Other times he has decided not to go out to church, which he normally loves to do, because he is feeling "foggy" or hasn't had a good night.

I wish I could have the conversation with him about what he wants to have done at times like this. The trouble is, he still hopes for a touch from God to take away this disease. He wants to live.... Who wouldn't, if they were well? I wonder if he would understand that I think the hospital would only prolong his life with LBD. I wonder if he would agree that his present state is not the picture of quality life. I wonder if he would feel like he has lost his advocate.

If God plans to heal him of this dementia, couldn't He also heal him of a stroke, or an infection, or any other life-threatening ailment? He could, and I am content to let Him (God) decide when those things come up, without outside interference. But what kind of caregiver, what kind of wife, does that make me? I'm just not sure. I think God and I are at peace with Him giving me directions for these scary moments. I will need a nudge one way or another. I will need help in not feeling judged for my decisions.

Yesterday I sat down with a cup of tea and a cookie. I thought and thought about these things, and all I could come up with, as I finished the last crumbs, was that I needed another cookie.

June Update

June 3, 2022
Hayward, WI

It's Sunday morning, and I thought we were going to go to church. After getting up very early, Dennis went back to bed and is sleeping again. I went in to wake him so I could help him get cleaned up, but he is sleeping so soundly that I have let him be.

He sleeps a lot lately. When he is done sleeping in bed, he sleeps in his chair. He sleeps fairly often when I am reading to him. He always listens with his eyes closed and looks like he's sleeping, but when he breathes heavily or snores, then I know he actually is. I wonder if this is a good thing or not?

I know it's very hard not to sleep when inactivity is the norm. He is so physically limited these days that he is weak and unstable when he isn't sitting or lying down. I asked him last night what factors were foremost in his slowness and sedentariness, and he couldn't really say and gave up trying. "I don't know how to explain it. Oh, well..." and the conversation was finished.

He passes on opportunities to go out more often. It complicates any trip to wonder if he will find a convenient restroom when it's needed, and when he has a hard time managing by himself. Everything is harder when he has to hold on to a walker, when he has trouble pulling up his pants, when he can't get the walker out the door.

Able-bodied people don't know how good they have it. No, they don't.

I recently read an article attempting to "stage" or give the phases of Lewy body dementia according to symptoms exhibited. It did not help me at all. He had symptoms in all phases except the last one before death. The only thing I appreciated about it was seeing the list of symptoms he doesn't have. I have no doubt that we are being spared the worst of it. Almost four years into our journey, and he still understands who he is, who his family is, and how to be reasonably himself.

Although things could surprise us and bring one or the other of us to a final end in a moment, it is looking like a long road to me. I need a plan for getting help, and that is what I'm working on now.

Caregiving

July 12, 2022
Hayward, WI

My senior assisted living community has gone down by two—a whole 50%. I still have the husband and Mom to help, but my uncle and aunt, both in their 90s, have gone south to live near my uncle's children.

They lived near a town about 25 minutes away out in the country, where we had trouble getting cell service. They had neighbors, but I was always worried about them being able to contact someone if they needed help. My aunt was disabled with Parkinson's and nearly blind. My uncle was the main caregiver for her and he was getting tired. On top of that, there was the difficulty of keeping warm and plowed out during our severe winters. Something had to change, and it did.

My aunt had a crisis on Friday, July 1st, and after a week in the hospital recovering, it was obvious that she needed nursing home placement. I was surprised to find out that there were no available beds for her level of care anywhere in our small community. None. But there was a place for her in a care center in the town where my uncle's daughter lived, and they were willing to accept her. I am in awe of the social workers who helped get this done so quickly that it about took my breath away. I also think it was God's plan to give my uncle some good time with his daughters after many years of just seeing them for occasional visits.

Caregiving... my aunt and uncle didn't require my time on any regular basis, but more as a problem solver and go-between with their doctors. I helped a little with their legal and financial affairs and often with their tech problems. Cell phones and computers drove my uncle to frustration. So, you would think I would feel free and have lots of extra time now that I don't have those responsibilities. I guess that's partly true—but I'm mostly aware of how quickly it all happened and how I miss them. Strange.

And that is one of the strange things about caregiving. It's often hard, restricting, physically tiring, stressful, and has distasteful elements, but it is also rewarding and more meaningful than a lot of other things I might be doing. Although I've been a paid caregiver and felt the weight of responsibility for my clients and the importance of being faithful and dependable, being a family caregiver is that and so much more. There are no 8- or 12-hour shifts, seldom a vacation, no weekends off, no differential for nights and no overtime. There are times when it feels like I'm handing over my life to someone else.

But it is my life, and I know I made intentional choices that determined my present circumstances. Like many other aspects of life, the challenge is in taking what comes to me and making something of it. I must make plans, but I must also expect the unexpected and figure out how to respond. I want to respond to situations in ways that won't make me disappointed in myself at some later date.

I guess preaching to myself is one of the ways I'm meeting those caregiving challenges. It helps me to remember that God has given me specific skills to use for the good of others, and that He will strengthen me and keep me in the game until I'm no longer needed. Knowing that I am in the right place, at the right time, for a good purpose makes me satisfied and gives joy. What more could I ask?

An Involuntary Trip

July 26, 2022
Duluth, MN

Things seem to go on forever the same, until they suddenly don't.

It was a pleasant summer evening. In an attempt to improve my own perspective, I was out having dinner with a couple of friends and my mom, in a noisy environment, when the waitress asked if it was my phone that was ringing. It was.

Dennis had been found on the floor by the helper who came to fix his dinner. She called my brother, and together they called an ambulance to get him to the ER. He had signs of a stroke.

I don't think he was on the floor for long, and he had no fall injuries. In fact, in the telling, he was very proud of how he had let himself down carefully so he wouldn't get hurt. Did I not get him an emergency alert necklace for times like this? Yes. It said, "Fall detected, press and hold to cancel." So, he pressed and held and cancelled. He's good at following orders. He was planning on getting to a chair, getting himself up, and recovering. He didn't want to fuss with outside help.

He was taken to the ER in our local hospital. They confirmed a hemorrhagic stroke with a CT scan and immediately called an ambulance to take him to a stroke center 90 miles away. I talked with him before they left. He didn't have severe symptoms—just some left-sided weakness and loss of skin sensation. Maybe his speech was a little difficult to understand, but he mumbled a lot anyway and this wasn't much different.

I followed the ambulance up and was able to see him safely established in his room, hooked up to all the necessary monitors. His blood pressure, which had been 225/135, was being carefully kept below 140/90. Another CT scan that night showed no further bleeding apparent.

Things had changed, suddenly. I always knew a stroke was a possibility with his blood pressure spikes, which happened frequently. He had stopped taking his meds because he had a period of relative stability without them. He didn't like taking pharmaceuticals, and I didn't argue with him since the meds seemed to make no difference. He was equally unstable with or without them. In hindsight, I wonder if we could have prevented this, but that is not to be known.

So, on July 26, 2022, Dennis traded his recliner for a $50,000 bed in a neuro trauma ICU. And this was just the start.

ICU Delirium

August 20, 2022
Duluth and Hayward

Dennis was admitted to the neuro trauma ICU of St. Mary's Hospital in Duluth, MN, 90 miles from our home in Hayward. It was past visiting hours, but after they got him settled in, they let me come in and see him. I watched them do neuro checks on him. He was weak on the left side, but there was movement, and his face didn't seem asymmetric. He was joking with the nurses, telling them all about how it felt. He was still on IV medication to keep his blood pressure in a safe range.

I stayed overnight with a friend and was back the next morning. Not much had changed as they tried various meds to keep his blood pressure low. Another CT scan showed there hadn't been additional bleeding from the night before. The free blood was kind of migrating around, though, like a bruise that changes shape as it ages.

Thursday, still in ICU, Dennis was more lethargic. He would open his eyes if asked, but he looked sick. They were having a hard time with his blood pressure and giving him higher doses of IV meds, as well as fluids and electrolytes. Friday when I visited, I had a hard time getting Dennis to wake up. He didn't interact with us. It was like he was sedated. It was explained to me that this was a common progression, as inflammation often peaked on the second and third days.

That night back at home, I got a call from the hospital. Dennis had been having a hard time breathing. And then, as they were suctioning to clear his airway, he actually stopped breathing. They intubated him and put him on a ventilator. I drove that night to my friend's house again, wanting to be close in case anything more happened. As soon as visiting hours started the next morning, I went to get the story. This was day 4 in the ICU. He looked very peaceful now that breathing was not so much work.

I couldn't begin to imagine what was going on inside his head. He was somewhat more alert, opening his eyes a lot more on days 4 and 5. He could still follow orders to move fingers and toes. The biggest difference now was that he could not talk, being intubated. I could tell there were things he wanted to say, but it was getting very frustrating.

As it got closer to our family reunion, August 4–8, people were arriving at home. I spent part of several days at home, but was at the hospital for hours every day. There was not much I could do except let the staff know, from experience, what Dennis was like and what I thought he wanted. There were conversations about resuscitation, feeding tubes, and DNR status that were kind of scary, but fortunately, I knew Dennis wanted to have every chance to live.

On day 7, my brother Gary and his girlfriend Lyn went with me. Seeing him like that was upsetting to them and frustrating to Dennis. He was very tired, and we didn't stay very long. Tubes and wires everywhere. Alarms going off. Phones ringing. Confusion of loud voices from the other half of his semi-private room.

We were starting to understand the term "ICU delirium."

Surgery

August 21, 2022
Duluth, MN, St. Mary's Hospital

Toward the end of the second week in ICU, after nine days voiceless with the endotracheal tube and the ventilator, it was becoming apparent that Dennis's respiratory problems were becoming long-term. To prevent damage to his vocal cords, it was recommended that he undergo surgery for a tracheostomy.

Having heard many scary stories of what general anesthesia could do to the mental status of Lewy body dementia patients, I was worried. But at least the surgeon listened well to my concerns, so we went ahead and had the surgery. It took longer than planned. The surgeon did say there was a bit of trouble, but the surgery was successful. Dennis's face was now free of the tube in his mouth and all the trappings to hold it there. Red abrasions on his cheeks and a very dry mouth would have a chance to resolve and heal.

However, the wound in his neck and the tracheostomy tube were pretty brutal-looking, too.

One of Dennis's main problems was that the stroke damaged his swallowing muscles. Secretions like saliva were not being swallowed down his esophagus like he thought. They were going into his trachea and his lungs, and there was danger of pneumonia. He needed frequent suctioning of the trach tube and of his mouth. Fortunately, he had a good, strong cough, and they started him on antibiotics to prevent pneumonia.

They tried several times in the next few days to wean Dennis from the ventilator. Each time it wore him out and he could only tolerate a few hours without the machine. Eventually, he was able to use less help—the vent was used more like a CPAP. He would initiate his breaths, but the machine would do the work of delivering the air. By day 24, he had been off the vent for 48 hours and was only getting humidified air and a little bit of oxygen.

One of the best things during these days was hearing him talk again. On day 20 in the ICU, they plugged the trach tube for short periods of time so he could speak to me. He wanted coffee—big discovery. One of the things about his brain injury is that he doesn't realize the seriousness of what has happened. He talks about wanting to eat and drink, not realizing that he is being "fed" through a nasogastric tube. I spent much of my time with him feeding him ice chips and then suctioning them back out again after they melted.

Things he has told me:

"If Ryan (son-in-law) were here, he could help me stand up."

"Untie my hand so I can hold a cup."

"Sweet corn and tomatoes!" (after hearing about his brother's garden on the phone.)

"My butt hurts."

"More ice chips."

"How is _____? (He remembers and asks about everyone.)

"I love you."

"When are you coming back?" (Aww...)

Out of ICU

August 23, 2022
Duluth, St. Mary's Hospital

Dennis was in the ICU for 27 days. I felt like I was there, too, and I was, nearly every day. Of course, the respiratory arrest and having to go on the ventilator were the worst complications of his stroke. The other important issue was his blood pressure, which was probably the cause of his stroke. That had to be stabilized to prevent another brain hemorrhage.

Unfortunately, unstable blood pressure has been one of Dennis's problems for a long time, and was probably one of his first symptoms of Lewy body dementia. The IV med he was given right away worked very well, but as the amount was reduced, he would begin to have episodes of hypertension again and it would be increased. Eventually, he was started on an oral med that was crushed and given through the nasogastric tube. When that didn't take care of the spikes, he was put on a second oral med. Then the amount of the first med was doubled. By his last day in ICU, he was taking Norvasc 10 mg, Coreg 6.25 mg, Ismo 10 mg, Cozaar 100 mg, and a diuretic, Lasix 20 mg—five medicines, all of which were for his blood pressure. Pretty impressive for a man who doesn't like to take pharmaceuticals. He still has a spike now and then, but it was decided that he could have a higher "normal" as long as it didn't result in 225/125 like it was on the night of his stroke.

Having been weaned off the ventilator and having stabilized blood pressure readings for a couple of days, he was given a second swallowing evaluation. He didn't do very well. That means he will be a long-term tracheostomy patient to protect his lungs. It means it is still not safe for eating or drinking, two of his only remaining pleasures in life. But medically, he was ready to move to a step-down unit.

Every change causes some measure of anxiety. For me, the worry was that he wouldn't be able to get help when he needed it on a unit with higher census and fewer staff. He still wasn't able to move either arm enough to find a call light. He wasn't able to move himself in bed at all. He couldn't turn his head to see anything he tried to locate, and he couldn't speak unless someone deflated his trach cuff and placed the PMV valve. He was often lethargic, but was becoming more aware of aches, pains, stomach rumblings, and the need to cough.

I was called one night at home and told that he had been moved to a medical unit on another floor. The nurse working with him informed me that he was on the same kind of monitoring as in the ICU, and had a private room with a camera that allowed supervision at the nurse's station. It actually sounded pretty good to me, and I was glad that he would be in a private room where it would be quiet and less confusing.

I visited the next morning and was very pleased with his proximity to the nurse's station and the attitude of the staff taking care of him. We practiced using a squeeze ball call system until he could work it correctly, and the PA directing his care gave permission for him to have the PMV valve in as long as he could tolerate.

There are always more mountains to climb, however. The PA also told us that his inability to manage his secretions meant that he would need a more long-term solution to nutrition and meds. The nasogastric tube could be replaced with a PEG feeding tube going directly into the stomach. This might also help his ability to swallow, since it would mean one less tube going down his throat. He and I both felt this would be an improvement, although it will mean another exposure to anesthesia. It will take place tomorrow. I hope it won't put him back into lethargy and brain fog, since we have just begun to make progress toward more wakefulness and clarity.

In the back of my mind is the question of where he will be cared for after hospitalization. They are already talking about nursing home placement, and I know this is not going to be fun.

Not Happening

August 24, 2022
Duluth, St. Mary's Hospital

Today Dennis was supposed to have a PEG tube for feeding inserted into his stomach—a procedure done in the radiology department under light anesthesia. It didn't happen.

I had explained what it was and why it would be better than the nasogastric tube he's had for weeks now. I played it up because I think having one less tube going down his throat might help him swallow better and eventually be eating and drinking normally. We were looking forward to having it done. By that, I mean Dennis was looking at the clock on the wall in front of his bed and asking every few minutes if it was time yet.

A few minutes before the appointment, a nurse came in and told us he had been rescheduled for the first thing tomorrow morning. They had several emergencies that took precedence. They were sorry. I was sorry.

Preparing for this procedure included having nothing in his stomach, so he had no feedings all day and the night before (via NG tube), no IV fluid, and no ice chips as he had been having before. He was feeling very dried up. Since his new appointment is early tomorrow morning, he won't be getting anything tonight, either.

All I want to say here is that we are getting used to disappointments.

All they mean is that we didn't know what God's plan was. We now know a little more about the next right thing He's doing for us. Accepting that does a real correction in my perspective. It makes waiting and trusting way easier.

On the bright side, today he was able to lift his right arm and bring his hand all the way to his nose to scratch an itch. He didn't think of doing it himself, but when I suggested that maybe he could, he tried. I only helped him a little. Later, he did it again to show the nurse that he could. He also shifted his upper body a little in bed, readjusting his position, which he has not been able to do prior to this. You may not understand why I am so happy about these small victories, but they are big changes in the right direction. Trust me.

I am praying that everything goes smoothly tomorrow. I hope to be up at the hospital in his room when they bring him back. It's been a while since I've seen his face without any tubes. I'm ready for that.

A Near Miracle

August 26, 2022
Duluth, St. Mary's Hospital

I know enough not to get haughty and demanding with God. On my walk yesterday evening, I had asked only for some small encouragement, something to keep us in the game and give us direction, some small arrow to shoot at the complex discouraging problems in view. I felt a plan was in place, even if I didn't know the details. I trusted we would be helped, based on the character of my God. And now I will acknowledge His actions on our behalf, because that is what is due.

When I arrived at the hospital on Wednesday morning, Dennis was already back from Interventional Radiology, and the feeding tube was in place. It had gone perfectly. However, the nasogastric tube was also still in place and would have to stay there, hooked to his nose, for another 24 hours before it could be taken out. We decided to allay our disappointment with a little work.

I fed him ice chips and started his exercises, moving every part of him that would move. He was just finishing this when PT came to the room. The day before, I had told the attending doctor that he had been alert all day and had scratched his own nose. He had talked to her and remembered her name. She had been impressed and had asked for him to be re-evaluated. The PT girls had him sit up on the side of the bed, and they, too, were impressed by his responses.

Then, Occupational Therapy came and had him brush his own teeth with a sponge stick, and a few other small maneuvers. Another point for the man. Speech Therapy came next and had him do a bunch of swallowing exercises. This was a busy morning for someone who had been nearly comatose for several weeks.

But wow, did it ever pay off! The attending doctor came in the afternoon and said Dennis was going to acute in-patient rehab at Miller-Dwan, the best facility in the area. It's connected to the hospital via skywalk. He would probably be able to go on Friday. Whereas he had not been a candidate for it previously, they now felt they had something to work with and were going to give him a second chance. I was ecstatic. Dennis was worn out, but I think he was catching on that a good thing had happened.

We talked about it (I talked about it) the rest of the afternoon as he practiced swallowing ice chips. So even though he still had the NG tube for another night, it felt like the day had gone gloriously well. He had been a trouper and had worked hard. I had been a good coach and advocate.

I left to stay overnight with a friend who lived a few miles away, feeling oh so grateful and amazed at such a turn of events.

To Rehab!

August 28, 2022
Duluth, Miller-Dwan Rehab

I thought the surprises were over, but they were not. Today, when I arrived at Dennis's bedside, I was able to see his face without the NG tube. The nurses had already taken care of that task. A good thing.

Dennis's face... he has lost weight in his face and looks so tired. The husband has very big eyes, hound dog eyes, you might say. When he looks at me or other people with recognition in those eyes, and maybe a lifting of the eyebrows in question mode, he sparkles with personality. When he has his eyes closed, or half-closed as they often are, he looks near death. He doesn't always show a lot of facial expression—it's one of the Parkinsonian traits of Lewy Body Dementia. Another feature of his face is the month-old beard and mustache. I've held off trying to shave him for fear some hair might be sucked into his trach tube.

The next thing we heard from one of the nurses was that he was being transferred to rehab today! Probably this morning! A day earlier than expected! His first feeding in the new gastrostomy tube was started, and a few minutes later, PT was knocking on the door to work with him. They were all excited and wanted to see if he could stand with their fancy lift machine.

The doctor came next, then the social worker who had been helping with placement. It was like a celebration with everyone smiling and congratulating us. It was like having a new baby, or maybe winning the lottery.

I actually felt guilty leaving before the move occurred. I had a much-needed massage scheduled and had barely enough time to get home for it. I've missed a lot of self-care lately (showers, haircuts, sleep, etc.) and decided that there were competent people who would take good care of Dennis during the transfer. And they did. I called this evening and he was in his new room, doing fine, according to the nurse.

Tomorrow I will have a new adventure, finding my way through a new facility, getting used to new regimens and rules. Dennis has always thought that trying to get well was his new post-retirement job, but I have a feeling this will be the most work he has done in a long time. The list of scheduled appointments is long.

His New Job

August 29, 2022
Duluth, Miller-Dwan Rehab

Dennis has a new job. I hope he's up for it because it won't be easy or short-term. His job is surviving rehab.

Yesterday, I made my way from the parking garage at St. Mary's Medical Center across the skywalk to Miller-Dwan Rehab Center. Finding my way in a new place is always an adventure. Knowing and following all the rules challenges me, especially since Covid. Hospitals are built with mazes as their model, and so many of the halls look the same. And it's not like they have a lot of restrooms for the public either. I drive 90 miles to get to Duluth, so I make it a point to find them.

A rehab hospital is an entirely different experience from an acute care hospital. I was so relieved at the quietness, low-key atmosphere, soft voices, and lack of hurry. The husband has a small private room with glass sliding doors, and it's right in front of a nurse's desk. He has a window and a nice bathroom. Since he still needs a lot of care, all the regular hospital extras are there—oxygen, suction, monitors and computers, lifts, and a fancy bed.

The social services worker assigned to Dennis talked with me, both to get information about our home situation for eventual discharge and to give information about his stay. We already knew he would be getting about three hours of therapy per day from physical therapy (PT), occupational therapy (OT), and speech language therapy (SLT). There will also be talks with psychologists, chaplains, social workers, and, of course, the doctors. They all meet weekly on Tuesdays and evaluate each patient's progress. The social worker promised to give me a report each Tuesday after their meeting.

At this point, they estimate Dennis will be with them for 60 days. I am not surprised that it could take a long time because Dennis is at zero on the independence scale right now. I am surprised and relieved that they are willing to take him for that long, as it will give me time to prepare for where he goes next. I am hoping our insurance will cover that amount of time. I haven't checked yet, and I guess that will be my new job.

No time was wasted by the therapists. They have all had two or three sessions with him during these last two days, mostly to evaluate and set up their plan. He is an exhausted guy, and it worries me to see him looking and acting so very tired. Before the stroke, he was walking, talking, feeding himself, and doing many of his daily activities without help, but I also have to admit that he was already tired and taking frequent naps. What kind of improvement can we even hope for now, given all that he's been through in the last four weeks? But this is humanly thinking, and I thank God that we are not limited to that.

I can tell that Dennis has had a lot of time to think, at night especially. He is often uncomfortable, or cold, or sore from his position, which he cannot change himself, and is unable to find his call button to get help. As his mind clears, he is more aware of his predicament and has started looking for someone to blame. He has landed on himself.

"If only I hadn't been so stubborn about wanting to do it my way. I didn't want to take those blood pressure meds. This is all my fault."

I did my best to talk him out of that one, reminding him that even when he took the pills, he had alarming hypertensive spikes, followed by hypotensive lows that nearly made him pass out. But I totally get what he's feeling because I also went down that road, feeling that I should have made him take his meds. It could easily be my fault, too.

When one of the therapists asked how far I was driving and how often I came, Dennis remarked, "I don't know why she stays with me." I had never seen him so despondent or heard him say anything like that before, and I was actually a bit shocked to hear it. The therapist didn't know what to say, and we had an awkward moment. Knowing Dennis always responded better to teasing, I told him I was sticking around until January because I wanted to be able to say I'd been married for 50 years. Did he laugh? I couldn't tell.

So you see, he is having to deal with some heavy emotions. He hasn't been one to admit to depression, even since the Lewy body dementia diagnosis. I am hoping some of the rehab deals with the natural depression that anyone would feel if they suddenly became weak, helpless, and out of control in every way. And I will be reminding him to look ahead as God guides him into a purposeful future.

Rehab Week One

September 3, 2024
Duluth, Miller-Dwan Rehab

Progress Points:

- New routines are getting in place at Miller-Dwan Rehab Hospital. OT early in the morning to get dressed, brush teeth, ADLs. Speech therapy. Off to the gym for an hour with PT and then back to rest. OT and Speech again in the afternoon. Evening rest.

- Off oxygen and still doing well

- Blood pressure remains stable

- No more finger pricks for blood sugar testing

- On a new mattress that avoids painful pressure points

- Allowed to sleep at night undisturbed if he doesn't need anything

- Beard got trimmed (yay!). Wearing real clothes during the day

- Having real conversations with the wife. Voice getting stronger.

- Getting "known" by staff

- Got to ride a stationary bike in PT, with help

- Room got personalized—the "love" poster from the family and all the cards are on the wall where they can be seen

- Sayings: When told rehabbing was his new job: "Take this job and shove it."

Rehab Week Two

September 9, 2024
Duluth, Miller-Dwan Rehab

All in all, a good week.

Today, after a morning of various therapies, Dennis was helped into bed and got a much-needed nap. As I watched him sleep, it was clear to me that he has improved. Even his appearance is more calm, less anxious, and peaceful.

The biggest change came on Wednesday morning when respiratory therapy came into the room and swapped his trach out for a smaller, less irritating Jackson trach. When plugged, it does not allow air in or out, making the breathing experience about the same as not having a trach at all. It is still there if difficulties arise, but if all goes well for at least 48 hours, it is safe to remove it and let the tracheotomy heal up. There have been no difficulties. Saturday morning, the trach is coming out and Dennis is so excited! It was the first thing he told me when I arrived this morning.

His voice has been clearer and easier to understand. He has not needed suctioning to clear his airway. He is moving his head and neck more, keeping a more normal position.

The progress on the physical therapy side is slower. He has continued to have low blood pressure when sitting and using the standing machine, making it hard for them to get him strong for those activities. Several times, they have cut the session short and returned him to bed to rest. There is progress, but because Miller-Dwan is an acute rehab facility, and Dennis's problems are more chronic, there is once more talk about moving him to a subacute facility to give him more rest time to get stronger. This makes me nervous, but I am grateful for all they have done, their good communication with both the husband and me, and the excellent treatment he has had.

They wanted to have the trach out before they sent him elsewhere, and I asked if they could also get him past needing the feeding tube. I am hopeful they will keep him another week. Social services will start looking for a facility closer to our home that could take him. I will start preparing our home in case there is no good place available.

In all this, I am not going to waste time and energy being fearful about problems we don't even know we have yet. I want God to know that I trust Him to work things out when we have the need. I believe He always has a plan for our ultimate good. The only difference from day to day is that sometimes we see how the plan is good, and sometimes we don't see—yet. His plan does not require me to be "in the know" at every step, and I clearly am not...

Sayings:

Nurse: "I need to take your blood pressure. Can I have this arm?" (the left one that he has trouble moving at all)

Dennis: "Yes, if you give it back when you're done. I hardly use it anyway."

Rehab Week Three

September 17, 2022
Duluth, Miller-Dwan Rehab

The trach came out on Saturday! He had no trouble, and the hole is healing up with only a Band-Aid on it.

Wednesday and Thursday were good days in PT and OT. He's tossing bean bags in a basket and sitting up by himself for most of the sessions.

The swallow test on Monday showed he is still not completely safe from aspirating, but he is coughing less during sessions with E-Stim (electrical stimulation). He had his first taste of ice cream on Friday.

He is more alert and engages others in conversation. He surprised a couple of people with phone calls where he did some of the talking.

On Tuesday of week three, I got a call from the social services gal assigned to Dennis. She reported that the weekly meeting of all therapists, nurses, and doctors had resulted in the decision to move him out, maybe by the end of the week. His progress was too slow to warrant the acute rehab aggressive schedule. He was often too tired or unable to focus for the whole session in PT. There were often issues with blood pressure and bowel problems this week as well. I understand what they are dealing with; nevertheless, the change from 60 days to "out by the end of the week" was a little alarming.

The next day, I went around to our local facilities in Hayward and got his name on their lists. There are three of them, and they are all full with long wait lists. But since we could be waiting for years yet, it was still worth it to sign up for something in town.

After social services investigated facilities that would offer the needed therapies within a reasonable travel distance, I was given the short list to consider. On Thursday, I decided to visit the one rehab/nursing home that had an open bed. It was in Shell Lake, 40 miles from home. True, that would cut my travel time in half on most days, but still… It makes me sad to be thinking of this level of care.

The building was acceptable and clean. The staff people who gave me a tour and spent time with me were pleasant and seemed candid about the quality of care given there. I felt it was a possibility, but was a little concerned about their ability to meet the needs of someone who can't even turn himself in bed.

Back at home, I happened upon a friend whose mom had been in three different facilities as an Alzheimer's patient. Shell Lake was the worst of the three. It was back in 2014, and things could have gotten better, but it did cool my already lukewarm enthusiasm a bit more.

I am praying that his progress toward the end of the week will cause the rehab team to reconsider and give him more days at Miller-Dwan. It could happen, right?

Rehab Week Four

September 27, 2022
Duluth, Miller-Dwan

Last Thursday marked the end of the fourth week in rehab at Miller-Dwan, one month of Medicare's allowed time. My schedule was the same, going up to be with the husband four of the days and at home for the other three. Here's what happened (in my experience, which is probably much different from the husband's).

He would try to wake up for his therapies, but I had a feeling something was "off." He was looking more like a nursing home patient than a rehab patient. A lot of vacant staring at nothing. Worrisome.

He kept his ability to sit by himself and correct his leaning. OT and PT did a lot of reaching and grasping exercises. Worked on the steps to roll over in bed.

My saddest day at the end of this week, I arrived and he told me he was trying to catch up on his sleep and not to talk to him. Granted, he'd had a hard night, and he did feel bad about telling me that later.

Maybe he's getting over some of his bias against talking to the psychologist assigned to him. I think he's understanding her role better. She's a good person to talk to, because she is willing to tell about her accident years ago, and the long time she spent in rehab. She's in a wheelchair, too. It's both sad and fascinating to watch her move around in her small office, which doesn't really hold us all very comfortably.

Shell Lake Health Care Center declined to take Dennis. They felt they didn't have the needed equipment and the ability to give speech therapy often enough. Back to searching for another facility.

Rehab Week Five

September 30, 2022
Duluth, Miller-Dwan

Last week, I was very concerned about Dennis. His behavior was as if he had "checked out." He wasn't answering when people talked to him. There was a lot of vacant staring and, even by his own report, his perception was altered. I wondered whether there had been another stroke or possibly the dementia had taken a turn for the worse.

It all made sense to me when they told me that Baclofen, a muscle relaxant that he had been given, was being discontinued. I did not know that the doctor had prescribed it to see if it would help his rigidity. There are side effects associated with that med that can really mess with the head.

At the same time, he had a bladder infection that was pretty significant and was being treated for that. Both the med and the infection could have caused the change in his condition. I was hoping when I saw him on Wednesday that he would show recovery.

Wednesday was a good day. He talked to me ALL DAY. What a difference! He participated in conversations with therapists and was so much more like the Dennis I knew. The therapies went well, and he was able to show progress in several different tasks. He was alert and not napping all the time. His speech therapist decided to do another swallowing evaluation, scheduled for the next morning, because he seemed to be coughing less and swallowing better. He was so excited about this. He actually wanted to watch TV, so we followed Hurricane Ian as it went through our former home area in Florida.

Thursday was not as good as we had hoped. The swallowing evaluation, 8:30 am, seemed to go okay, but when we reviewed the results at noon, we were disappointed. No progression to a diet yet. He is still losing fluids down his airway and is risking pneumonia. Therapy will be continued along with tube feedings. However, the other therapies went well, so there were enough interesting moments to be thankful for. I was surprised to see him successfully guard himself from a beach ball tossed in his direction. He can move his hand quickly enough and with good aim to bat it away.

He has become very emotional. I can tell when the "cry face" is starting, and it just about breaks my heart to see him affected that way. This is a long, tiring road, and the ups and downs are like a roller coaster.

We pray together each day when I leave, and that is his most emotional time. The tears flow when I remind him that he heard God say, "That's my boy." And for now, we are still at Miller-Dwan, where he has come to know and love the staff members who work with him.

They are still looking for a long-term facility where he can continue therapy, but none has been found. On to week 6...

PART SEVEN: WE CHANGE OUR HOPE

Thoughts at Night

October 7, 2022

So many thoughts come when I'm awake at night, usually waiting for a headache to resolve, praying because I cannot sleep. Those times are not necessarily bad, even very sweet once in a while.

People come to my mind, one after the other, and I realize how rich my life is with a wide variety of friends. Circumstances come to mind and I realize how complex the world is. Everywhere there are situations that make people suffer and cry. Some say that God, if there is such an entity, should step in and make it different. I've read in the Bible that it was different once, in the Garden of Eden, and the people of that time, Adam and Eve, chose to trust their own decisions instead of the wise instructions they'd been given. Turns out that has been a prevailing trend ever since.

I'm amazed that there is so much hope, beauty, and encouragement left in the world, and it often steps into view when we need it most. That is not an accident. It's the plan, to lead us back to the way it was, eventually. No one but an all-powerful God is going to bring about a world that we will all want to live in. It's too far beyond any world leader or government. I am encouraged because I see evidence of His forethought and control everywhere in nature. The question becomes, how then shall I wait?

What hope do you have if you cannot imagine there is a God who could be wise enough to solve our problems, who could dissolve the anger and hate in hearts, who could comfort the inconsolable and bring justice to both sides of every equation?

It is arrogant to think that because we cannot imagine something, it cannot exist. Our search should be for a better, more faith-filled imagination.

So Fast

October 15, 2022
Duluth, MN/Superior, WI

When things happen... they can happen fast. (Maybe too fast. Maybe before we are ready.)

Mom went with me to the rehab hospital yesterday. We were watching the speech therapist spoon-feed applesauce to the husband when the social worker appeared at the door and beckoned me out.

After weeks of searching for a bed for Dennis, something closer to home and less aggressive in therapy, there was an opening at St. Mary's Hospital in Superior. It was only a few minutes closer to home, but it was across the state line in Wisconsin, and that was an advantage for future placement. There was medical oversight, since it was a hospital, and they had the therapies that were needed. It was called a "swing bed," and most hospitals have a room or two of that category for patients transitioning to a different level of care.

I don't know if I had a choice—it didn't really feel like it. I had not seen the place nor had I heard anything about it. But that didn't last long because several staff members started telling me they had worked there and it would be an excellent move for Dennis. I was uncertain, but it seemed wrong to refuse to have him go. I must have agreed, yeah, I must have. Otherwise, how could it have happened that fast?

Two hours later, he was on his way over to his new room. Those two hours were pretty unusual, though, and Mom and I were so glad we were there to witness them. Every one of Dennis's therapists, nurses, and aides who were on duty that day came by his room and spent time saying goodbye to him. With each one, he would tear up, then they would tear up, and all of us watching would start to cry, too. Two hours of emotional mess. Exhausting.

They all had stories to recount of Dennis's jokes, his cooperative spirit, and his progress. They were a hugging bunch. It couldn't have been a better send-off for a man who often felt like he was failing and being a burden.

I'm going to say, and believe, that it must have been time. God knew we were completely ignorant about the new facility. He knew I would be uncertain. He knew we would trust Him and go, and that He could be present with Dennis in that place just as he had been for the last 50 days at Miller-Dwan. We pronounced it a happy thing and prayed with Dennis before leaving to have dinner with some friends.

We checked in on him on our way home after he had been settled in bed for the night. I'm not going to say that everything looked ideal, but it did seem adequate, and I felt he would be well attended.

Has he made progress since the last update? Yes, he did some good work that last week at Miller-Dwan. He is getting more control of his hands and arms, more fine motor coordination, and wider range of movement. He became better at sitting upright and centered. He was able to rise to a standing position with the help of a steadying machine.

Yesterday, his last day of therapy, a therapy dog came to the gym for the first time since Covid restrictions. He had such a good time tossing the ball for "Gunner" to retrieve. I just hope he can maintain these advances in the new place, and that will be my prayer.

Grandfather's Clock

October 31, 2022
Superior, WI, St. Mary's Hospital

It was the afternoon of October 13 when the husband left Miller-Dwan for his new, but still temporary, bed a few miles away in Superior, WI. He's had two full weeks and three days now to settle in. He's met new people, gotten used to a new schedule, new practices, and new surroundings. All of this newness would be hard for any of us if we were entirely dependent on others. Dennis has borne it well, maybe better than I have. He continues to do his best without complaint.

Because he wants to be done with the feeding tube and get on solid food again, the work he does with speech therapy to improve his swallowing is important. One of the first things the therapist did with him was to repeat swallow tests with observation through a fiber-optic camera. I got to watch, and they reviewed the results with both of us. It is amazing to see vocal cords in action and all the different components of a swallow. We who swallow without giving it much thought have no idea what a marvelous design is involved. Think about it—a shared entryway into the body where both food and air have to be maneuvered and timed so as not to interfere with each other.

Unfortunately, the test showed that it still would not be safe for him to start eating any kind of food or drink other than ice chips. It's disappointing, but he is still working hard to strengthen those muscles with therapy four or five days a week.

The "swing bed" that he occupies is in a small hospital of about 20 beds. Surgical patients come and go. Because of that, the therapists' schedules vary from day to day. They spend roughly half the time with him that he was getting at Miller-Dwan. He never knows when they are coming to him and whether he will have energy left to work with them. There is no concerted effort to get him dressed every day or to make sure that he is out of bed a certain number of hours. Staffing is often short—nurses are not sitting somewhere waiting for call lights to go on. They are quite occupied.

In spite of all this, the care is still good. The people are compassionate, kind, and competent enough, and thankfully, Dennis does not need anything very complicated now.

He has had a number of new visitors in the last two weeks—friends from the past, from our church, and family members. These times are always emotional for him. His affinity for tears continues.

One day, my friend Pam was visiting him while I was at home. I texted and asked her to tell Dennis that I would not be coming up the next day because I had made some appointments. He wanted to know what appointments. She had to relay to him that I was getting estimates for our funeral and burial plans. He then gave her one of his famous "deer in the headlights" looks, as if he did not know that needed to be done. But I will admit that it is a weird thing to attend to, even when you know it's necessary.

In addition to his practiced looks, Dennis has taken to singing frequently to caregivers as lyrics come to mind. The last couple of days, he's been thinking about the song "My Grandfather's Clock." It's about a clock that stopped when its owner died. He sang the first verse from memory today while Mom, my brother Bob, his nurse, and I were listening. He was crying, but managed to get the words out. Truth is, we were all crying, even the nurse. She kissed the top of his head and hugged him. All this to say that he is getting to people and they are seeing the gentle sweetness in him as he faces a seemingly sad and uncertain future.

And because he always tears up now when I leave, it is hard to walk out that door. As we were preparing to go today, he said, "Oh, I hate to tell you the song I just thought of, and I don't like that it came to mind." Of course, we had to know what it was then, so, crying, he belted out "Hit the road Jack, and don't you come back no more, no more, no more, no more." On that note...

Moving Again

November 8, 2022
Spooner, WI

It's been 23 days in "swing bed" status at St. Mary's in Superior. The husband has become accustomed to the people, the environment, the routine. So, naturally, it is time to change things up again.

Thursday, November 3: The care conference with the case manager and therapists in Dennis's room, with me on the phone, was concerning. The physical and occupational therapists have noticed that he has trouble remembering steps and sequences for moving. He doesn't seem to be able to build to a greater skill level because of that. He heard this report, and later, when I questioned him, he agreed with their assessment.

The goal with these physical therapies has been to make transfers possible without mechanical help and multiple people. Dennis has muscular strength, but he doesn't know how to direct it when it comes to complicated (yes, complicated!) movements like standing up or sliding over. He has reached a plateau. They feel he should transfer to another long-term facility. His only remark was that it should be as close to home as possible. However, there are no beds available in Hayward.

Friday, November 4: By the time I reached the hospital parking lot, my plan for the day got scrapped. I got a call that there was a bed available in a town 30 miles from home. I had not visited this facility, but decided to say yes to it, pending approval after I had seen it. Dennis and I discussed the move. He's already dreading leaving this batch of new friends...

It is so confusing to navigate the rules of Medicare. If it were not for the social workers and case managers that we have encountered, I would not know what to expect. They are very good at keeping track of how many days are left at different levels of care, and how to keep Dennis getting some more time with the therapies he needs most.

One of the most improved areas lately has been his work on swallowing. He has steadily increased the time on the E-Stim device and the number of swallows he takes. I am glad that the speech therapist made sure he got one more evaluation with the fiber-optic camera, and it did show improvement. He was given the choice of having some soft foods like pudding if he was okay with the slight risk involved. But there is still more work to be done before he can consider having the feeding tube removed.

Tuesday, November 8: I visited the new facility in Spooner yesterday after my time in Superior with Dennis. It was neither greatly good nor greatly bad. It's hard to be specific about what makes some places clearly "nursing homes" and other places "hospitals." Sometimes it's the fact that many nursing homes are in older buildings, abandoned for their original purpose or dated in some other way.

Maple Ridge Care Center is a former hospital with several wings off a central nurses' station. There are parts of the building that are completely unused. One section has been made into a daycare for the employees' children. The outside of the building and the grounds are neglected, sidewalks and curbs cracked and crumbling, the foyer sports a rumpled rug at the entry, and leaves and debris have blown in from outside. Doors in the hall are open, showing offices with varying degrees of mess and disorganization.

The better aspects of the facility were the people working there. Many of them were young and appeared competent. The patients were mostly sitting around in wheelchairs, watching birds in the small aviary or playing bingo in the dining room. Therapists were wheeling people back and forth after their sessions. It looked busy and fairly happy.

The room where Dennis is most likely to end up was large and empty. Some painting or repair had taken place, and it hadn't been refurbished yet. I could see it being a nice room, although it was in the long-term wing instead of short-term rehab. I'm not sure if there is a message in that, probably not. I hope they are getting it ready today since he is scheduled to leave Superior at 9 a.m. tomorrow.

I will try to be there to meet him when he arrives—they have open visitor hours 24/7. They also have some Covid patients they keep in quarantine. They evidently aren't having too hard a time with the virus. One other concern about Maple Ridge is that I've noticed it's hard to get anyone to return a phone call. I will have to train Dennis to pick up his own phone when he gets there.

November Update

November 16, 2022
Spooner, WI, Maple Ridge Care Center

Freezing rain, snow showers, cars covered with dirt and salt spray, gray skies, darkness, all coming before we are ready for it. It's definitely November in Wisconsin. My daily trips to Spooner seem short by comparison, but they are still challenged with this weather.

I am learning how different a nursing home is from a rehab hospital—something I knew in my head, but experience emphasizes it. Some days, I am dismayed with the care the husband is given. Some days I feel much better about it. Several days, I have had to wake him up and get his care started without help. The weekend was actually frightening with the staff being stretched thin and several incidents happening. I wasn't sure Dennis was getting his meds or his feedings on time or at all.

Today, I arrived late in the morning, and all was peaceful and calm, the room was straightened, and my husband was dressed and sleeping in his recliner. But let me tell you about yesterday…

Somewhere between his speech therapy session, which I was told went well, and his PT session, something happened to Dennis. He was much different, being unable to participate in his PT transfers, unable to keep himself upright, and not being responsive to questions and general talk. He stiffened and was hard to move and slept for hours without his usual requests for position change or the urinal. I wondered if he was having a second stroke. After a couple of hours without improvement, it was decided to pack him up and go to the hospital ER for evaluation. The ambulance came and got him.

I will mention here that he didn't want to go and had to be talked into it. He saw nothing wrong with the way he was feeling. I knew something wasn't right, but didn't know what. I'm the one who has to think about him needing emergency care. Emergency care in the nursing home amounts to an LPN doing chest compressions while waiting for a phone request for a doctor to show up—no monitoring, medications, or personnel familiar with running a code. I pretty much scared him into going by telling him to get evaluated or risk dying in his bed.

At the ER, we got so much information over the next five hours. He had a urinary tract infection, but the good news was that he didn't have Covid, didn't have pneumonia, and didn't have a second stroke or heart problems. He got a dose of antibiotics in his feeding tube and another ride back to Maple Ridge in the ambulance.

I went home and was settling down to sleep when the nursing home called to say Dennis was on the way back to the ER because his feeding tube had come out. I had heard a popping sound while watching the ER nurse give the antibiotics. I assumed she was familiar with the different ports on his feeding tube. I even asked her about the inflation port for the balloon that kept the tube in place in the stomach, hoping that she hadn't put the med in that one. She didn't seem concerned. The popping sound had been the balloon breaking. Somehow, the tube stayed in place all the way back to the nursing home. It didn't slip out until back at the nursing home when they moved him about.

So back he went to the ER. Dennis got a new tube put in and two more rides in the ambulance. What a night. And, as I said, he is pretty hard to wake up again today, but for a good reason.

I find it hard to sit and watch him sleep. He is unable to wake up long enough to focus on anything or communicate more than a word at a time. I hope that as the urinary tract infection clears up, he will revive, be himself again, and resume therapy.

Our setback matches perfectly with the gray, wet, coldness outside. It's November.

No Place Like Home

November 22, 2022
Spooner, Maple Ridge

We have not been here before. The husband's experience with Lewy body dementia has been atypical—no hallucinations, personality changes, severe memory lapses, or all the other nightmarish things I read about in online support groups. But this stroke and subsequent hospitalizations have taken him down.

It was reasonable to think that he might recover some or all of his pre-stroke abilities, as other stroke victims do. And he did. He got back to breathing unassisted, verbal communication and basic movement, and strength in his arms and legs. He was motivated to work hard and was able to express that. He talked to friends on the phone, gave feedback, joked with caregivers, and noticed his surroundings.

Even a week ago, he responded to the move to Maple Ridge pretty well. Then came the day I wrote about last, when his lethargy increased and he went nearly comatose. This was the first time a urinary tract infection had affected him like this, something I have read about countless times in the support groups. The day after his two trips to the ER, he was started on antibiotics and given a new feeding tube, so he was understandably tired but seemed to rally a bit. He was cooperating with the therapists. We played catch with the beach ball.

Yesterday and today, he is once again silent and not communicating. I have to work to stimulate him enough for his eyes to slowly open and stare at me. A wet washcloth, touching his face, turning up the hearing aids, sitting him up in the bed, deliberate and focused speech—all this gets very little response. He is stiff, rigid, and difficult to position in bed. There is the perpetual lean to the left that he's not able to correct as well as he did a week ago.

What happened? Am I seeing the dreaded progression of dementia? Are we on the Lewy roller coaster? Or is the inconsistency of his care at the facility having something to do with his condition? Will he go in and out of this behavior, or is it permanent? So many questions, so few answers.

I'm talking and thinking in the language of this answer-less world all day. I recount the day's happenings to friends, my mom, my daughters, my brother, my pastor, even the nursing home employees who will listen. I'm telling God what it's like to sit and look at this shell of the man He gave me. I'm constantly going back in my thoughts to this situation we are in.

If he has declined because of the inconsistency of his care, then I need to bring him home. I can be consistent, if nothing else. If he has declined because of the progression of his diagnosis, then I need to bring him home, because these may be his last days. Either way, the comfort of being home and of having someone respond to his needs will be the best thing for him. He deserves more than what he is getting now. I think I am ready to bring him home.

Preparation

December 1, 2022
Spooner, Maple Ridge

It's the first day of December, and in honor of the new month, I want to move forward and record our next adventure. The last four months since the husband's stroke have been full of hospitals, rehab, and nursing homes for him. For me, it's been hours in the car traveling to keep an eye on his condition, his progress, his caregivers. I've spent very little time at home and didn't feel like doing much when I was there.

So, that's all changing tomorrow. I can't believe tomorrow is nearly here, at last. We will be packing up and leaving the nursing home at 2 pm to travel the half hour to our home at Par Place. Some of our transfers took two hours from start to finish, but for some reason, this one has taken ten days. I have been pushing and being the "squeaky wheel" the whole time—ever since I became convinced that Dennis would be better off and happier at home. There have been obstacles in our path, and one after the other, they have melted away.

The new life, well, I debated whether to call it new or more specifically, different. The different life for me will be staying at home and being a full-time caregiver. Hopefully it will give Dennis some consistency and more attention.

However, there is the question of whether or not we can actually do this as well as we would like. I've put a lot of thought and effort into getting equipment, supplies, formula for his tube feedings, and helpers. Most weekdays, I will have help for two hours in the morning and two hours in the evening. I have friends who will come and give me breaks for exercise and appointments around town. But he is quite helpless, weak, and often disoriented. All his meds and nourishment have to go through the stomach tube (PEG tube). He is bowel and bladder incontinent. He will have to be moved with a Hoyer lift from his bed to his recliner or wheelchair. He sleeps most of the time. Fortunately, he is still himself on those occasions when he wakes up and talks. He knows me and his friends. He remembers that he is coming home on Friday.

So, because this may be the last thing he and I do together, I want to remember how it went, what we said to each other, and how it felt to know that life might very well be coming to a close. We have talked some about these things, but only recently has he at last confessed that he couldn't think well enough to be in charge of his own health care. "I trust my wife," he told the hospice nurse.

Although we had the conversation and an evaluation, we won't be getting help from this particular hospice. As a private, for-profit hospice, they won't accept him as long as he has a feeding tube, sorry, but those are the rules. I was upset for about five minutes and then remembered that God had been asked to lead and direct, and He is faithful. I was able to adjust and be relieved that Dennis wouldn't have to be affected by their rules. That decision was out of my hands.

To write and remember in December, that is my goal. So, more tomorrow. I'm sure it will be an exciting day...

At Home

December 3, 2022
Hayward, WI, Home at Last

Because no damage was done, I will start with this event, which I found somewhat humorous.

Before I got to Maple Ridge yesterday, I received a call which started, "I need to tell you what happened yesterday afternoon." That's not usually going to be a good report.

As it happened, someone had left the control for the lift recliner where Dennis could find it. He often feels that making the chair go up and down relieves the burning sensation on his backside. This time, it did more than that, as he lifted himself up and slid out of the chair.

They had to pick him up off the floor with the lift. There were no bruises or pains as a result, and he looked fine to me when I arrived. I was grateful nothing had ruined our departure, which took place a couple of hours later.

They called all the staff over the loudspeaker to come say goodbye. Evidently, that is a common ritual for this kind of facility.

A very resourceful friend found a tilt-in-space wheelchair for us—for free, no less. This made it possible to go home in a wheelchair van, which was much less expensive than a stretcher by ambulance. The thirty-minute trip was uneventful. I'm going to say that the driver left the minute we went through the front door at home because he didn't even want to get asked to help. Not that I would have asked him.

The reality of being alone with my helpless husband had a hint of panic associated with it, I admit. But I hooked him up to the rented Hoyer lift and promptly found that it did not lift him high enough to easily leave the wheelchair. Another discovery was that he was not going in his beautiful recliner where I had envisioned him spending half of each day. It was too wide for the legs of the Hoyer to fit around it. It wasn't a situation quite as bad as someone having to lift a car off a trapped passenger, but I was surprised that I was able to get him on the side of the bed, unhook the Hoyer, and finally get him straight and lying down. Surprised and tired. It was interesting how he was silent, bent nearly double in the sling, during the whole event. I think God has blessed him with limited awareness of any of the situations he's in.

He and the cat "re-bonded" immediately, which was very nice to see. He also requested coffee with cream as soon as I had raised the head of the bed.

The rest of the evening was spent putting things away, trying to remember where I had put the things already put away, figuring out the medication and feeding schedule, and meeting a new caregiver who came at 6 pm for a couple of hours. More about that another time.

Since I had never spent a night with him since his "healthcare incarceration," I did feel the need to sleep close by so I could see how he behaved. That is to say that I did not sleep much but spent most of the night listening to various levels of gurgling and snoring. I think I have learned that he remains quite still and does well when the head of the bed is raised. I believe he had a good night's rest, but I decided not to ask him just in case. It was enough that he remained alive after his first night at home. We did it.

Week One in the Living Room

December 7, 2022
Hayward, Home

We are nearing the end of our first week with Dennis being at home. A routine is developing. Our helpers are arriving on the assigned days. Every day we figure out some small thing that is a better way of doing, a better product, a better schedule, a better order. Hard things become more doable.

I am so grateful for all of this. There is a certain comfort having the two of us in the house, three counting Shadow (the cat). Our times are quiet. The sun comes in through our living room windows on a clear day. The moon and stars, reflecting off the snow, light up the still nights. We help Dennis to sit in the recliner (a smaller one) where he sleeps or listens to TV or music. The cat settles down on his lap in the chair or on the bed. There is some little chore every hour or so, a medicine, feeding or position change.

The more active parts of the day are getting going in the morning and getting to bed in the evening. There is about an hour of work involved making sure the husband is clean, dry, and comfortable. It's physically taxing for us caregivers and for him. He gets exhausted being lifted, rolled, and "fixed" for whatever is next.

He says very little and sleeps, or has his eyes closed, most of the time. He says he has no pain, no fear, very little discomfort ever. He can answer simple questions like that, but ask him anything complicated and he cannot find an answer. He has nothing to say about any of his care, with the exception of an occasional joke.

There is evidence that he is not a blank slate. He dreams a lot and talks in his sleep. He asked yesterday if I would read something he wrote "in the Spirit." He was very proud of it and said it was a lot like what the Founding Fathers would have written, Ben Franklin in particular. He said it was kind of about politics and the need to be a good listener, that silence isn't necessarily weakness. It took a while for me to get all this from him by asking questions. I wanted to know how I was to read it if it was "in the Spirit," and the conversation got too complex at that point. He stopped and admitted it was confusing, to him as well as to me.

I am glad that he does not seem to be suffering or unhappy—those are complicated thoughts, and he just doesn't have them. I think it is God's blessing on him that he doesn't have the awareness of his own condition. He is not a complainer now, although that used to be one of the family's sore spots. In the past, he was more prone to notice one thing not to his liking and disregard a host of commendables. His nature has softened, and he has become more reflective, accepting, and content. He has been very open to God moving him in that direction. It is one of the blessings that has come.

One thing yet to be figured out is how I will find my own life around the demands of caregiving. At this point, I spend a lot of time staring into space and trying to be ready for the next task. Trying not to run out of supplies, trying to remember medication schedules, trying to be creative in making our time together interesting, good. But it is winter, and there are very few expectations of me. My stress is limited to caregiving. That also is a blessing, and I am grateful.

Crazy Talk

December 9, 2022
Conversations in Hayward

Dennis: "I'm working on the remote control for my fan, the VMPK." *(Holding his hand in* the *air as if grasping something)*

Me: "Do you remember that you are retired? You don't work for Aldes anymore."

Dennis: "But I'll take this in. I have it figured out."

Me: "Why do you have to do it?"

Dennis: "Because it's my invention." *(He remembered that correctly)*

Me: "There are other people working there now. They are carrying on for you. You haven't been going to work for four years now."

Dennis: "I need some coffee to help me think. Can you get me some pigeon fulminator?"

Me (*incredulous):* "Some what? Pigeon fulminator?"

Dennis: "Yes. It's a fruit. It's all around you on the shelves."

(*Me, laughing—him looking embarrassed)*

Me: "You made that up, didn't you?"

Dennis: "No, I didn't make that up. It's a fruit. They grow it in someplace like Hawaii or the Philippines."

Me: "So you think it's in the grocery store?"

Dennis: "Yes, it's all around you." *(pointing to my face and around)* "There's something like a blow torch on the shelf, too."

Me: "Why are you touching my face?" *(As I lean over him doing morning care)*

Dennis: "I'm picking a peach off your chin. There's a nice bowl of fruit, and I would like some. With cereal."

At night, when I came out to find him uncovered and chilly in bed. He had been calling a name—two syllables with an eeeee at the end. I assumed it was Shirley.

Dennis: "Who are you?"

Me: "I'm Shirley, your wife. You were calling me."

Dennis: "No, I was calling Julie."

Me: "Well, I'm the only one here, so I came. It sounded like my name you were calling, but you aren't talking clearly."

Dennis: "I was saying Julie, not Shirley. I'm cold and need a blanket."

Dennis was in the recliner in front of the TV while sermons were on TBN. I asked him if he was okay, if he was cold and needed his arms covered up. He began talking about all the animals in a mumbled sort of monologue.

Dennis: "…all those animals on the ark…"

Me: "You mean like with Noah and the ark?"

Dennis: "Yeah, that's a lot of animals, and they need to be organized and put in the right place."

Me: "Is there going to be another flood?"

Dennis: *(he laughs)* "No, I don't think so. I was just thinking about the Hoyer lift to get some of the animals on."

Me: "They couldn't just walk up the gangplank?"

Dennis: "After walking all that way, it would be hard. They're tired."

Me: "And the Hoyer lift would work to lift them up?"

Dennis: "Yeah, it would."

Me: "Did you just hear something about Noah on the TV?"

Dennis: "No, I'm just thinking about it."

Restless

December 13, 2022
Hayward, Home

It's hard to describe how someone can be apparently sleeping, and at the same time be restless. Isn't sleeping rest? Good question. We are starting to experience something that doesn't feel like sleep or rest for either one of us.

The last couple of days have brought a few subtle changes. The husband did well at keeping his eyes open while we had visitors, but he could not talk. Later, he tried talking to me, but I could not understand him. Much of the problem I attribute to his mouth being dry. He breathes with it open all the time, and his tongue dries out and becomes pretty useless in forming words. He doesn't move his lips, either. Words are just a bunch of vowels—aahh, eehh, uuoohh. I guess and we play 20 questions until I give up.

And then the restlessness started. I stopped dressing him in sweatpants for convenience's sake, instead putting a blanket over his legs when he sat in the recliner. But it wouldn't stay on. One leg would come up on the chair and the blanket would end up on the floor. Twice, when the recliner was fully extended, he got his legs trapped between the footrest and the chair and couldn't get out. That was interesting.

Then I started finding him uncovered in bed whenever he was in it. It does get warm in the house on a sunny day, so I can understand him wanting to cool off. But at night it can be chilly. Last night, every two hours or so, I found him with the sheet twisted around his feet, his bare legs and shirted torso uncovered, blankets on the floor, eyes wide open, and hands reaching for some invisible something. One time while I covered him, he said, "Cover me more," and it came out clear as a bell.

So my guess is that his lucid moments are becoming fewer, and his "dreams" or hallucinations are more frequent and require movement. So he moves whatever he can, which is mostly his right leg and arm.

I know I've been losing him in small increments for a long time, much of it he has hidden. He's not able to hide anything now.

These are the sad times that I speak about. The good thing is that he is here with me. I don't have to go anywhere to take care of him. No snowy, icy roads. I can handle the interrupted sleep and the crazy talk.

White Winter

December 14, 2022
Hayward, Home

Today we have a snowstorm in progress. We must be on the edge of it because there is very little wind, just a lot of heavy, wet flakes. The temp is just above freezing, making the roads hazardous. Our caregiving help has the morning off because I did not want them to travel the 20 miles to us.

I put Dennis in the recliner (I feel like a 3-year-old, "I did it all by myself!") and pushed him up to the living room window. He had his sips of coffee and is sleeping again. I have been outside making sure the bird feeders are full and taking pictures. It is a beautiful snowfall, but I am afraid it will break some limbs off the trees. Sitting together, watching the snow—what a gift it is.

Monday, we had a video visit with our primary care doctor. I am so thankful that virtual appointments have become a thing done well. I guess we have the last few years of the pandemic to thank for that. Our visit with her resulted in our second attempt at getting hospice help. There are at least two hospice organizations in our area, and soon to be a third. Some are "for-profit" and others are not. Apparently, being refused by one does not mean refusal by all. Medicare guidelines do not exclude patients with feeding tubes, and we do have a local nonprofit hospice.

One characteristic of hospice is the speed at which they respond.

Monday afternoon, I got a call from a nurse and an appointment for Tuesday morning.

The nurse who evaluates incoming patients and her trainee spent about an hour meeting at our house with us yesterday. They left saying that it was possible for us to get on their program, and they promised to get back to us after presenting it to their superiors. Again, they will look at Dennis's need for a feeding tube in order for Medicare to grant payment. I guess whether or not it happens is not very important to me anymore. I've chosen the path we're on, and I know we can handle it without their help if we have to. It will be okay.

I have heard from so many family members and friends in town and far away, and thank God for all the prayers and words of encouragement. Daughters Julie and Esther are making plans for a visit in the next few weeks. Dennis's birthday is the day after Christmas. Our 50th anniversary is coming up in January. I have so much to look forward to! A kind neighbor sits with Dennis and allows me to get out for appointments and a walk now and then.

I am finding ways to take care of myself so I can take care of Dennis. So many people have been encouraging self-care, and I hear them. As a nurse, I have frequently said it myself to others and I know it is important. I think I'm doing well on that account.

Most important are the prayers people are praying for us. It means so much to know that our God is hearing our names mentioned to Him by others. The accumulated effort of His people is influential and carries weight with God. It's not that He needs a magic number of prayers before He can take action—He is always acting on our behalf, and we feel unusual favor in all the places we've been. But I believe He is delighted when His people act like they have gotten His point—we are here to learn to love each other and care.

Miraculous healing is not the point either. It's sometimes a wonderful encouragement and evidence of God's power, but what we are promised is that we will die of something in this imperfect world. I'm okay with God deciding when and how. He knows so much and makes the best decisions! That's how I look at our situation, and I know Dennis agrees with this, too.

Accepted

December 18, 2022
Hayward, Home

Accepted. The husband. Into hospice.

The last four months have taken their toll on Dennis. I have been convinced that he would never have gotten through another hospitalization. However, having that thought did not prepare me for the feeling of signing a paper agreeing to not have resuscitation. It's the DNR document, and hospice requires it. It came with a lot of emotional weight.

The last time Dennis was able to talk about the subject of hospice, he was agreeable to entering the program if it would help him get home from Maple Ridge. He also thought a long while when the hospice nurse asked him if he felt he was capable of making complex decisions about his health. He finally said no, he didn't feel capable. Being too tired to think very long, and sometimes confused and disoriented, he was still realistic enough, and brave enough, to say that he trusted me to decide for him. Since then, he's become more confused about his own condition, often forgetting that he's had a stroke. Often he forgets that he hasn't been getting up and walking to the bathroom. He forgets he hasn't been eating for months and has a feeding tube.

More often now, he is living in his dreams, sometimes with eyes wide open, hallucinating. His hands shoot up while he's lying in bed, and he's reaching for… who knows what? But each day there are a few good moments when he is oriented and involved with his real surroundings.

Today, sitting up in the recliner, he was watching our YouTube cooking show from Azerbaijan. It's slow-moving with country scenes, animals on the farm, and a very proficient farm couple harvesting food and cooking some amazing dishes. No talking, no fast-moving ADHD programming. He perked up and watched and recognized things. He wanted some coffee—the only thing he asks for that I can give him, besides tea. We sat together enjoying the show with me giving him spoonfuls of coffee every now and then, until I noticed he was asleep.

Have you ever really looked at your spouse's teeth? Not just the ones in front, but all of them? I thought I had, kind of, but now that I'm helping brush them, I realize I didn't know what's in there. In fact, his whole face looks so different now. The musculature is changing, being held differently. It's painful to watch him change, but here we are. Changing, ever changing.

Beginning the third week at home.

Democrat Cookies

December 18, 2022
Home in Hayward

Dennis: "I would like some (unintelligible word) cookies."

Me: "You want to have a cookie?"

Dennis: "I want some Democrat cookies."

Me: "Did you say Democrat? Democrat cookies?"

Dennis: "Yes, Democrat cookies."

Me: "I don't know what those are."

Dennis: "Well, you just said it."

Me: "I said it because you said it. I don't know what a Democrat cookie is."

Dennis: "The kind they serve at parties."

Me: "I don't know anything about those—is it a particular kind? I didn't know there was such a thing, or Republican cookies either."

Dennis, after a moment's thought: "Well, I'll just have some coffee then, without the cookies."

Last Day of 2022

December 21, 2022
Home in Hayward

Most every year, during the month of December, I carry two planners around with me. One is for the present year, and one is for the year to come, because I am often planning ahead. That's what planners are for. The last day of December often finds me closing out one and looking back over the fading year. I am doing that today.

The first half of this year, I often wondered how Dennis's diagnosis of Lewy body dementia would play out. He was obviously experiencing symptom progression, but so slowly. I thought he was dependent on me in some ways, but little did I realize that being able to walk at all and being able to eat are very independent activities. He was still doing those things at will, and amusing himself during the day with TV, phone calls, and books.

The stroke took all of that away. What followed was 25 days in ICU, 5 days in a step-down unit, 49 days in acute care rehab hospital, 26 days in skilled care rehab, and 24 days in a nursing home. I've been sitting here with my planner, counting up the days and marking the events. Most of these places were 90 minutes away from home. The last was only half an hour away. I've put thousands of miles on the car. I was weary of traveling and welcomed bringing him home. This is his 29th day at home, the 17th day under hospice care.

I am the primary caregiver, although we do have around 15 hours of care each week from CNAs hired privately. That is the summary of the second half of 2022 for the husband and me. It's been a year to remember.

I can't say that I have felt like writing much during this time. Occasionally, it has been an emotional release. I might also like to have a record of what we have gone through, at some later date when memory fails me. But much of it I would like to forget. Ten years ago, I would not have imagined living the life I have now.

Should I say something about God and His part in the road we're on? I see Him as having been very patient and understanding of my fatigue, my not wanting to think deeply, or pray consistently, or immerse myself in Scripture every day. In some ways, I am numb to those disciplines in much the same way as a young mother with a house full of toddlers would be. God sees what overwhelms His humans. He sends me out to the woods on a "walk and talk," and I will tell you that the natural world has been my lifeline this year.

He sits with me when I cry. He gives me words for the husband when calming and encouragement are needed. When action is called for, He has given me the thought of what must be done and the energy to do it. He has given me assurance about all the confusing and uncertain things—that I can trust Him and decide not to fear, not to blame.

Many friends have said they are praying for us and have reminded me of that often. That has weight with me. This is not the first time that prayer has been important to me, but still it is a mystery how God uses it. I want to be involved in that mystery, not necessarily to understand it, but just to have a part in it. Somehow God attaches great power to prayer, and I love to see Him be powerful, up close and personal.

I think it was good that we asked God for healing for Dennis. Why would we not? But it is also okay that he has not been healed because perfect health is not the only blessing God can bring with a hard experience. And we have always known that we will die at some time—it's just the end part of being human. We will not waste the experience by becoming bitter or turning away from the most exciting relationship humanity has ever been offered. No, neither Dennis nor I feel any disappointment with God, or the way He has exhibited His friendship with us.

He has been "with" us. Sometimes, He has been a peaceful presence on my walks. Sometimes, He has sent others to us to spend time or offer help. I'm often told that I'm not alone and have felt like saying, "Well, I feel pretty alone in spite of what you say." But now I receive that differently. God puts that sentiment on the lips of others to remind me that He is with me, even when people are not. That's enough. He is not named Immanuel, "God with us," for no reason.

PART EIGHT: UNFORGETTABLE DAYS TOGETHER

Fifty Years

January 14, 2023
Home in Hayward

Fifty years, somewhat the worse for wear, but we have made it. We have experienced, often enjoyed, sometimes survived (barely), and definitely been blessed by fifty years of covenant marriage. Our covenant was with each other and with God. God's part was, and still is, HUGE.

Back in 1973, we had no idea how different we were, in temperament, in interests, in long-term goals, in relationship language. We were in college, where our similarities were highlighted. We liked music, we actually went running together, we took time for dating, we had few responsibilities except to do well in school. We each had spent time in higher education—Dennis already had his PhD in Physics, I was partway through nursing school. At this point, we both were aware that we were looking for a marriage partner. We were realizing that our growing relationships with God were making it hard to find people we were comfortable with. I have always thought that was the reason God brought us together. That desire to share a serious faith in God was at the top of the priority list. In that, we were well-matched.

So, for each of us, God helped the finding, the deciding, and the living it out. These years have shown us how we differ, for sure. I have often wondered why God thought we could make it, but He knew things we didn't and was willing to help us, change us, and grow us.

The man God chose for me is a very unusual and interesting person. Because of who he has been, I have never worried about infidelity, being impoverished, never been threatened by addictions (unless you count addiction to work), and never dealt with meanness or deliberate selfishness. During tough times, I knew that we were both counting on God to teach us and help us through. God was always pointing out options, and none of them were ever divorce. I am so grateful.

Today, I am not sure this husband of mine knows it is our anniversary, our 50th. He is severely disabled and at home with me in hospice care. How hard this must be for him, and yet he is uncomplaining. He still exhibits his love for God, for music, even for me. He doesn't remember much about where he is or what has happened to him, but he remembers who to call out for when he's confused.

I remind him he can still talk to God, even when that's all he can do. I tell him that we are not in China (and have never been), that we are in Wisconsin, that our condo is a safe, pleasant place, that the living room is now his bedroom because his hospital bed doesn't fit anywhere else. He says okay, and for a while, he is fine with all that. He says that if I turn off the TV and the lights, he will go to sleep, and puckers up for a kiss.

A couple of months ago, I told him he had to stick around until January 14th, so as not to cheat me out of saying I had been married 50 years. I was uncertain he would make it. This morning, we have spent precious minutes going over that day 50 years ago. He remembers the snow falling and who was his best man. Today, his memory is clear, maybe better than mine. Funny how that works. Happy anniversary, husband. Happy anniversary to us. We made it.

Caregiver's World

January 26, 2023
Home in Hayward

My husband is in the last stages of Lewy body dementia and can no longer do anything for himself. He is in hospice care at home, where I am his main caregiver. This is my world.

One of the biggest changes for me after my husband's stroke was accepting all the things I could no longer do. When he was still able to manage by himself, I could do music at church, volunteer with my favorite organizations, and meet with others for exercise. Since the stroke, and after bringing him home, I can't leave unless I have a sitter to be with him. I have to prepare him ahead of time by giving him his feedings and medications before I leave. I can't be gone for more than three or four hours max—usually only two.

That's enough time to get groceries or have an appointment at the auto dealership for an oil change. It's enough time to do paperwork at home or a cleaning project. It's possibly enough time to take a much-needed nap. But it's not enough time for me to mentally leave my caregiver world and be involved in others' lives to any extent. It just isn't. I've started losing touch with my community and feeling isolated.

But time has added new skills. After six weeks with my husband at home, I'm finding new, small ways to get involved that don't overwhelm me or cause more stress. This week, Mom has joined me and we are volunteering, from home, for one of my favorite organizations, Northwoods New Life Resource Center. We are helping with a fundraising campaign. It's the perfect, low-stress activity. I have frequent contact with others and get to be involved in a great cause. Volunteering from home, what an idea!

A big anti-isolation factor for me has also been learning to utilize the helpers I pay for and the ones that come with hospice enrollment. My hired company gives me two morning hours and two evening hours each weekday and every other weekend. Now that we know each other, my daily helpers let themselves in and tell me to get lost. I use the time to shop for groceries, pick up prescriptions and other odd errands, or I go over to spend dinner time with family. My hospice volunteers give me a couple of hours more in the middle of the day, once a week. I want to use this time to find out if I can still remember how to ski—it's a bit sketchy...

Hospice has also been a blessing because of the number of people who come to us in an average week. The husband and I see the weekly volunteer, a nurse, a CNA, a chaplain, and a masseuse (she works on the caregiver, too, yay!). We've gotten some good conversations and some new friends.

As hard as this time is for the husband and me, there is no sense in adding to the sadness by letting ourselves feel isolated. Separating from meaningful activity and our caring community only hurts us. We don't have to let that happen, and we won't.

Supplies

January 28, 2023
Home in Hayward

I pay close attention to the mail these days because that is how much of my shopping for the husband gets done—online and arriving in the mail or by UPS or Fedex. Packages come frequently to keep my little, private hospital supplied. What I'm learning is that I need a purchasing agent.

When I first knew that I was going to have Dennis at home, I searched medical supply companies for the items I knew he was using in the nursing home. I could never find them all in one place, so I ordered from three or four different companies. I have since become overwhelmingly confused with passwords, promo codes, and "did I really order this?" syndrome. One day, a whole case of disposable briefs came when I thought I had cautiously ordered one box to make sure they were the right size. I'm never sure what's coming anymore, but it's entertaining that way, and I need entertainment. I pay for the privilege of being surprised.

But my biggest shopping woe has been finding the husband's nutritional formula. He gets everything through a feeding tube. His formula is calculated to supply all his nutritional needs. I found a company that had it, but after three weeks it was out of stock and I had to find another supplier. It's relatively important not to run out of this stuff, so I get pretty nervous when I'm down to only a few bottles. The second company has also started sending me messages about stocking problems.

Yesterday, I was down to a one-day supply when two cartons showed up. One had traveled about four different places since starting from Pennsylvania on January 13th. The other had come from Florida and only been traveling for four days. The packing slips didn't have recognizable order numbers, although it is all from the same company. I'm getting so confused. At the end of the day, I know I've been charged for two more cases, and they are probably out there seeing the world on their way to me. I'm hoping to pray them in. In an emergency, I guess he could have what I eat without starving, but I don't know if popcorn would blend up and go down the tube very well.

I have just put the husband back to bed after several hours in the recliner. Getting hoisted up in a sling evidently isn't the most comfortable ride because he starts doing a little half-moan, half-song during the process. I think he's self-soothing by distracting himself, but who knows. He doesn't tell me what he's feeling, and most of his songs have no words. Except the other night, when I was telling him about the cooking show we watch on YouTube. He decided to sing the word Azerbaijan for a while—that's where the cooking show is from. I took it as proof that he's listening to me even when pretending not to.

That's all for today's look into my caregiver's world. It gets a little crazy.

Where Am I?

```
January 30, 2023
Hayward, WI
```

"Can we go home?"

"Where am I?"

"What is this place?"

These are some of the most frequent questions I'm asked this winter. The husband has been home since the beginning of December. Each time the opportunity comes along to orient him, I tell him how he's been sick for six months and in several hospitals and a nursing home, but that he is now at home.

"We are in our condo in Hayward, and you are in our living room. You are in a hospital bed because you are too weak to walk. You have a hard time swallowing and are fed through a feeding tube into your stomach."

It is all news to him. Sometimes these things register, and other times he just closes his eyes and says nothing. The next time he has to go to the bathroom, that's exactly what he thinks he can do. He needs to be reoriented all over again.

I tell him, "You can't get up. You aren't strong enough to walk and haven't walked for months."

He tells me, "How do we know if you won't let me?"

I tell him, "If you could walk, you would be up doing it because I'm not stopping you."

This exchange is about as feisty as he ever gets. He has the same co-operative nature that he has always had, but the cognitive decline is very noticeable.

Lately, the neurological decline is more apparent, too. There are times when he cannot speak clearly, or at all. Other times, he can suddenly have a conversation and be understood. What he's saying may not make sense, but I can tell what the words are.

There are some nights that I think he's dying (nights are always the worst times), but the morning comes and things look different. His body is stronger than his brain. If he gets an infection of some kind, things could change quickly. I try to be careful in caring for him—in the complexities of enteral feeding, medication administration, watching for skin breakdown, and managing incontinence.

It helps to have hospice on the journey with us. I don't have to make decisions alone in most cases. It helps to be able to hire help, to share the heavy lifting and the unpleasantness of necessary tasks. God has supplied a wealth of resources in all areas of need, and that is good because this might be a long haul.

Some details:

- Dennis is on three enteral feedings daily, about 8 hours apart, which amounts to a 1200-calorie diet. He does get hungry, and that looks like restlessness. When I see that, I know it is time for a feeding. A full stomach is very soothing for him, and it puts him to sleep for several hours.

- His blood pressure has been stable on the three blood pressure meds that he gets twice a day.

- He's had a UTI recently and been on 3 different antibiotics. One was finished when we found out the culture indicated two different ones. Lots of bacteria are getting killed.

- Most of the day is spent sleeping in his mother's La-Z-Boy recliner, with an occasional awake moment in front of the TV. He might be listening to much of what goes on. There is occasional evidence.

- The rest of the time, he is in his hospital bed in a variety of positions. He goes back and forth between these two places with the help of Harvey the Hoyer. Dennis decided on the name, and it gives us a good laugh.

- Our paid caregivers come on weekdays for two hours in the morning to help the husband get into the recliner for the day and for two hours in the evening to get him prepared for the night. Every other weekend I have help, but we are working on that. I'm still filling in the day and doing the nights. It's interesting and sometimes exhausting, but when I need to, I get sleep.

- We are grateful for the humidifier that runs 24/7 in our dry winter climate

- Our daughters visited recently and were able to connect with their dad in good ways, mostly through songs. He still remembers and comes out of lethargy to sing when coaxed. Thank you, Esther, for the humidifier, and Julie for the seemingly endless supply of cookies to cheer my soul.

That's all for this update.

Being Contrary

February 1, 2023
Home in Hayward

Today, in my caregiver world, things have not gone as expected, but have not gone badly either. For one thing, I did not make my bed, and it set the tone for contrariness for the whole day.

The CNA coming to help with morning chores needed to hurry and be done, and it was unfortunate because I was needing her to stay with Dennis while I went to my study group. I called on my brother, and he was able to come, but it was a bother to have to come up with another plan. I was able to get to my Bible study group late, but I was there. My phone only disturbed the group twice before I had to leave—early. Why did I bother going at all? I spent some time thinking about why it is so easy to stay home in contrast to the effort required to go someplace.

One of the phone calls led to a new piece of equipment getting delivered today. The hospice nurse thought the husband would benefit from a suction machine, and it was added to our little "hospital at home." I worked with it and we tested it together until he said, "Don't do that anymore," after which he called me from another room to suction him again.

But while we were doing all this, I started watching a YouTube video that I could not get away from. I was fascinated as I watched this young Asian girl carve a homestead out of the tropical jungle, all by herself. She chopped bamboo, carried rocks from the mountainside, built substantial structures to live in and house her animals, got her gardens growing, and even wired the place with electricity from a turbine set in the stream. She was so smart and good at all of it. She pounds nails without bending them or hitting her fingers. Her channel is called Ana Bushcraft, and she was very crafty.

I didn't always know what she was building, but I could not stop watching her work. Her patience and willingness to do things the slow way with whatever materials she could find made me wonder if I would be able to work like that. One project at a time, she transformed her part of the jungle. It was nice to lose myself in her world where there were no sick people, no meetings to attend, no technologies or devices to drive her crazy—just a lot of plain old hard work. (But I also wondered who was behind the camera, out there in the rainy jungle day after day.) It rivaled the other channel we watch—the cooking show from Azerbaijan.

It was probably a little wasteful of my time, but as I said, I was feeling contrary. I should have been making my bed, but it will be a lot quicker to get into tonight. I'll make it again tomorrow.

We Step Out

February 4, 2023
Hayward Hospital ER

It was Thursday night and I was getting ready to meet a friend at a restaurant for dinner. Dennis was back in bed after an afternoon in the recliner. I crushed up his evening pills, dissolved them in some water, and took them over to pour them in the feeding tube. It was about time for our hired caregiver to arrive and for me to leave.

I hooked up the syringe/funnel to the husband's feeding tube and poured medicine in and watched as a wet circle appeared on his shirt. I checked my connections with alarm and couldn't see any leaks or openings. Then I lifted the shirt and discovered the real cause. The other end of the tube was no longer in his stomach.

There it was, with the balloon that was supposed to keep it in place mostly deflated. I didn't know when it had come out, or why, but it probably didn't take much to bring it out. Something like this had happened before when he was in the nursing home, and it resulted in a trip to the Spooner ER for tube replacement.

I seriously entertained the thought of sticking the thing back in, and would have tried if I had known I could inflate the balloon to keep it in. I didn't have the right kind of syringe to do that, so I followed plan #2 and called the hospice nurse. Let someone else decide...

I also called Grete and asked to postpone our dinner to another day, knowing that it might take a while to see this circumstance to a satisfactory end. I also called the caregiver and told her we most likely would not be home. The husband and I were stepping out for the night.

Hospice called the ambulance for me, and they were soon at the door. Dennis knew enough to be a little anxious, but I reassured him that we were going on this adventure together. He laughed. I like that he laughs at my jokes a lot more these days. "Adventure for you," he said.

After our short ride in the ambulance, we were introduced to our ER crew and gave them the story. You have to understand that after a tube like this comes out, something should be done very soon to keep the tract open. The PA attending us knew that, but unfortunately he had never encountered this problem yet and didn't think they even had another gastrostomy tube in the ER. Luckily, I had brought the old one along in a Ziploc. That's what they ended up using.

It wasn't easy to get it in, but after several attempts and a couple of techniques, it was replaced and the balloon inflated. I'm a little worried that there might be a slow leak in it and we might have another event in the future, but so be it. We were discharged and back in the ambulance for the ride home within three hours. That is amazing for any trip to the ER.

The husband got pretty tired out, but I think he kind of enjoyed the extra attention, meeting new people, new places, all that. Isn't that what we hope for on "date night"?

Note to self: Get one of those feeding tubes before the next time—I bet they have them on Amazon.

Our Lewy World

February 11, 2023
Home in Hayward

I spend a fair amount of time wondering how long this disease is going to hold my husband captive. He seems now to have entered that world of vacant-eyed, non-communicating persons who can't answer questions anymore. "Do you hurt anywhere?" is too complex a question for him. He has the rhythm of speech and a searching look as he makes sounds. Every once in a while, a real word escapes. It always surprises me that it has nothing to do with a relevant topic. Off the wall, almost off the planet...

I do the things for him that I know I should, not knowing if they are the things he wants done. Does he want to be left alone? Does he want to be bothered and stimulated? Is he listening to us as we talk around him during his care? How does he feel about our routine? So many questions.

As I look at him and think about all the different stages of life we have been through together, I feel so sad. He would never have imagined this helpless, brain-damaged state for himself. Who would?

It has been a roller coaster progression. Those days when he is more alert, showing that tiny bit of himself that is recognizable—those days are fewer now. This week, he produced the smallest hint of a smile when asked. I hugged him one night, and he put his hand on my back and patted it. It was so sweetly familiar it made me cry.

All these thoughts and more swirl around our daily activities, our routines. It is probably a blessing that we have things to do, the husband and I. Useful work anchors our souls in the present, instead of wondering about the future.

Here is our present routine, in case you are curious. The day starts for me around 4:00 am. On a good night, he has slept for hours in the same position and needs to be turned and put in dry briefs. He has also been without a feeding for long enough that he acts restless, which I interpret as hunger. A feeding of formula in his tube quiets his stomach and puts him to sleep again like a sedative.

I take the audio monitor and go over to Mom's condo for coffee and conversation. I come back in time to crush and give the morning meds, again through the feeding tube. Our caregivers arrive around 8:30, and I like to have my own breakfast done by then. For two hours, I can either work with them on some of his more complicated cares, or I can leave to do errands, or maybe even spend time outside on warmer days. They leave by 10:30, and Dennis is up in the recliner for the next five or six hours. The change in position does him good, although he sometimes thinks he is still in bed.

During his "up" time, I find videos or TV programs for him to listen to. He seldom opens his eyes to watch things, but he is often listening. He sleeps a good deal of the time. He gets another feeding around 11. Workers from hospice do their weekly checking during this time. His RN comes on Tuesdays, the CNA on Thursday mornings. The chaplain has checked in with us, and a volunteer comes once a week to give me free time for a couple of hours. I busy myself with daily laundry, ordering supplies, basic housekeeping, and caring for his physical needs until around 3 in the afternoon, when I help him back to bed. I move him with a Hoyer lift, which makes it pretty easy, but it does require some experience. Thankfully, I have had years of that with a former client.

His third feeding of the day comes at about 4 pm. Feedings are a mixture of 200 ml of water and 300 ml of formula, given by gravity feed. It gets put in a bag and hung from a pole like an IV. Getting the formula has been a problem, and I get messages that it is out of stock all the time. Several times I've been down to the last bottle before another shipment comes. That it always does come in time has been one of the ways that I've been assured God is aware and caring for us.

Another slew of crushed pills comes at 5 pm. The evening caregiver arrives at 6 to give me another break for dinner. They help get Dennis comfortable for the night before they leave at 8. He gets his last feeding of the day at 9 or 10, depending on how tired I am and how badly I need to sleep. I do go to my bedroom to sleep, but I have the monitor and can hear how he is breathing. I get up and check him at least once, more if he's having issues.

I record all these happenings, as well as doing blood pressure checks, and giving frequent oral care. I would probably consider it a pretty easy nursing job if it were not 24/7, and if it were not my own dear husband. I have to shut some of the sadness out, or it would be too much.

Changes will come, but for now, this is my caregiver's world.

Two Hours of Normalcy

February 21, 2023
Hayward, Backroads Coffee

I have heard that normal people often go to coffee shops to sit and connect with the world over unsecured internet and drink expensive coffee. I needed to try this during my two hours of freedom today.

For some reason, I have a hard time thinking of things to do when my hospice volunteer comes for her weekly visit with Dennis. I haven't yet found the friends who are free during work hours to do things with, so I end up going to Walmart for groceries and prescriptions and whatever excitement Walmart provides. I need to do better. I would like to make Tuesday free time a treat, a time to do some "normal people" stuff and have fun. Spend money someplace other than Walmart.

There is one standalone coffee shop in our small town, and I admit I was a little worried when I got to the parking lot. It was parked up pretty good. I knew I was taking a chance to do this on Birkie week, when thousands of skiers show up to do this ridiculously long cross country ski event. But it is early enough in the week, and the town is still in the preparatory stage. The coffee shop had empty tables and I am sitting at one, drinking my medium chai, having a scone, and writing, of course.

I'm enjoying watching the activity outside as the street is getting marked with "no parking" signs. The temporary bridge has already been erected over the main highway where the skiers will cross over and head up Main Street for the finish line. It is such a fun winter event—one of several claims to fame that our town enjoys. Winter storm Olive is due to make it even more interesting this year. I would love to be volunteering at the food tent as in other years, but I'm also glad to be staying home. Staying home is what I have to do, and being content with what I have to do is my main winter goal.

Being content is a worthy pursuit. It takes a little practice, but so do most good things. I will not always be in this season of having my husband to care for. Being content leaves me free to look around, enjoy this moment, really notice people and things around me. I enjoy sitting and not wanting to be anywhere else. I'm looking at the people going in and out of the shop and guessing whether they will be skiing the long race or not. I'm aiming prayers at them, hoping their experience will be safe. I'm praying that as they ski through this beautiful northland, they will sense God and wonder at His creation.

The scone is gone. The chai was good. I found four hundred seventy-five words to express how it feels to be normal today.

Remembering

March 2, 2023
Home in Hayward

Conversations with the husband are rare these days. He often talks at length, unaware that his speech is unintelligible. Most of the time, his control of speech muscles is minimal, but there are those exceptional times of clarity. It is then that I get a glimpse of what his mental status is.

Today I went over to him because he seemed to be restless, and I thought a little re-orientation would be helpful to calm him. We talked about his memory and who he remembered. I asked him if he knew who I was. He did.

"You're my wife."

"Yes, and I have two rings on my finger. One of them is yours."

"How many rings have you got on?"

"I have two rings on my finger. You see this?" (holding up my hand)

"Yeah, I see that as four fingers."

"Yep, and see the rings on that finger?"

"Yeah."

"One of them is my wedding ring, and the other one is yours. One of them is the diamond that you got for me, and the other is your wedding ring that they took off you at the hospital. They were afraid your hands would swell up and it would be too tight."

"And what ring of mine are you wearing?"

"Your wedding ring."

"Oh yeah. (pause) Are you married to me now?"

"Yeah, don't you remember we got married?"

"No."

"Well, how did I get to be your wife if we didn't get married?"

"Oh, yeah."

That was only one of the interesting exchanges today. Earlier, he told me that another "me" came in the room from his left and joined the "me" standing at the bedside, and I was transformed into someone even more "me."

If only the other me's were able to help out a little more, maybe I could get some rest. Wishful thinking...

Night Conversations

March 28,2023
Home in Hayward

"Shuree, Shuree."

"Shuree!"

I woke up suddenly. It is 1:00 a.m., but it's not very often he actually attempts to call my name, and I can't wait to hear what is happening.

"My pillow." (*said in his soft, thick-tongued voice, which sounds almost like an accent. He never sounded like this before.*)

"Oh, your pillow is on the floor! You lost it. Is that better?" *(after arranging his head on the pillow again).*

"I'm hungry," he says, as he reaches for my hand.

"Oh no, and I've already given you extra before bedtime. I can give you some water, though, and maybe a little "food" with it, in the tube."

I warm up the water and take the leftover formula out of the fridge, load the bag and prime the tube, hook him up, and start the drip. He wants to talk more.

"Are you happy?" (*Something he's never asked before*).

"No, not really. I'm sad that you're sick."

"I'm not sick."

"It seems like you are, but are you happy?"

"Yes, and I want a cup of coffee. Can you make a cup of coffee?"

"We don't usually drink coffee in the middle of the night when we want to sleep."

"It would make me very happy if you would make me a cup of coffee."

(I can't believe he's asking this in such a sweet, almost begging manner. Of course I will make him some coffee. I do the Keurig thing and take it over to him. He has a spoonful.)

"You can take a sip," he says.

"I'm going back to bed when we're done, so I'm not going to have more. I took a sip just to make sure it wasn't too hot for you."

"I called you here to see if you could make sandwiches for the men."

(*This is an odd twist, and I'm not sure where it's going...*) "What men?"

"The men out on the street. I thought maybe you had sandwiches in the freezer and we could give them some."

I remind him that he called me to get his pillow and because he was hungry, but he remembers none of that. After I tell him again about the stroke and how his body doesn't obey his brain anymore, he tells me I'm exaggerating. I recount the months since he's been unable to walk, eat, or do anything for himself. He stops talking, and I ask him why—it's because I'm arguing with him.

I can tell the feeding is making him sleepy. He says his stomach feels better. I tell him that it was nice of him to think of hungry men on the street and want to feed them. He had about four tablespoons of coffee during our conversation, so I put the rest away, cover him, and turn out the light.

Happy Birthday to Me

April 8, 2023
Home in Hayward

Today had a nice start to it. After going for a coffee at Mom's, I returned to Dennis and started our morning routine. I usually ask whether he wants to get up in the recliner, even though I make the choice myself. I think it's good for him to be more upright for a while, and it also gives me a chance to change the bed linens if they need it. Today he said "yes," and it was because he wanted coffee. Coffee is the only drink he gets, other than mouthwash and water, and it evidently is tied emotionally to normal life in a very important way. He asks for it often, even though it only amounts to five or six spoonfuls before he is tired.

As we sipped our coffee, I told him it was my birthday and invited him to say the greeting to me. He said it clearly, and I was thrilled!

"Happy birthday."

"Oh! You are really talking good this morning!"

(A surprised look, as if I would ever think otherwise.)

"So, since it's my birthday, what month is it?"

"April."

"And what date is it in April?"

(After a long pause, which I thought might never end) "Eighth"

Again, I was amazed at what he can dredge up out of the usual garbled and confused jumble that his mind has become.

Unfortunately, these times are happening less and less. Dennis often has episodes of anxious behavior. Loud, rapid breathing, agitated hand and foot movements, and some loud vocalizations occur even though his eyes are open and he seems awake. He hands me imaginary things and asks me to put them in the box. He joins in a conversation when the other caregiver and I are talking, and I assume it's something relevant to what we're doing, but no. He wants to know if I've cooked salmon, or if I'm ready for the representative from Rhode Island to visit us (*what?!*). And it's often the dog that told him to say that—the dog we don't have but he sees right there in front of us.

A couple of nights, I've treated this confusion with sleep medicine, but I have to wonder if he's more confused after he wakes up. He's also having signs of pain, which he mostly denies feeling. He calls out loudly and pulls his legs up. Today, after one loud outburst, I asked him if he felt pain, and he finally said yes. I asked him where the pain was, and he said, "My heart." This is new. I'm not sure how accurate his evaluation is, but it is significant if only because he is usually denying any pain.

I'm getting very tired. Daytime naps are now a must.

The Dog

May 6, 2023
Home in Hayward

As his imaginary world becomes more entrenched, the husband is always asking me where his dog is. He mentions this dog at least once a day, and this morning it wasn't just a curious inquiry; it was a need.

It was early in the morning, and he was being moved and cared for, but it was upsetting to him. The words were quite clear. "I need my dog." It was repeated with conviction. "Where is he?"

I have gone the route of explaining that we don't have a dog, but that he has seen a dog in his mind, and that's okay. That doesn't seem to help lately, so I have begun telling him that the dog is probably outside, since it is not in the house. People take their dogs out in the morning—they have to pee. His dog does, too. He wants to know if I can see him, and I say no. I tell him not to worry because he has told me himself that the dog is very smart.

Eventually, he will ask for the cat. I can produce a cat. He will hold Shadow on his lap and feel her, and this morning he settled down. I am grateful that she does cozy up to him and sit on his lap quite often. She is little and black, like "the dog."

My theory has the dog being important for several reasons. The husband needs unconditional love at a time when he knows he is unable to give back. It also comforts him to feel responsible for a creature, to still have purpose. Lastly, I don't know, maybe he always wanted a dog when he was young and never had one. He has always enjoyed some things about the dogs we have had in our years together, but he didn't have the need that he does now.

His condition continues to decline. I feel there is less engagement overall. There is more confusion, more resignation. One morning last week, I asked him if he was okay, as I often do when he's had a coughing spell or seems upset. "Not really," he said. He has also started asking me, "Am I confused?" These are new admissions for him.

Lest you think that he does a lot of talking, I am recording here most of the significant conversations, and there aren't many of them. He doesn't usually talk when we are working with him. His eyes are closed much of the time. He unfailingly produces a smile when asked. Every now and then, something will make him laugh. This morning, when I told him the dog was outside "taking a leak," as he calls it, he laughed and said, "We're doing the same thing together."

They were, and that's okay.

Two Dreams

May 30, 2023
Home in Hayward

Dennis often told stories about dreams God had given him and how important those dreams were in his LBD journey. I cannot tell how many times I heard him recount the dream God gave him early in his diagnosis. In the dream, he and God were talking about his research, the books he was reading about dementia, magnesium, and a cure. As he often did, God gave him only one word. Dennis didn't understand the connection between the word and his disease, but he was curious and knew God meant for him to investigate, so he headed off to the laboratory. On his way, he looked back and saw God smiling and saying, "That's my boy."

Knowing his status with God carried him through the toughest of times and enabled him to trust. He was a scientist, an educator, a thinker, a researcher, and God loved him that way. He never doubted that God had spoken to him, even when he wasn't sure what God meant.

Ever since the stroke and the entry into advanced medical care, we have done everything we could think of to slow or reverse this disease. When asked about resuscitation in the ICU, Dennis said he wanted to live. He wanted every chance to recover from the stroke. We continued in that mindset through the months of rehab. I was still in it when he came home. Even signing the DNR papers as part of our entry into hospice didn't change my perspective.

And now, I've had a dream. In it, God reminded me that I wasn't just a victim of circumstances, bound to a seemingly endless life of medicating, feeding, and suffering with someone I loved. He reminded me that Dennis had stated his wishes about prolonged life, specifically on a feeding tube, when there was no hope of recovery outside of a miracle. He had put me in charge of the decision if he could not make it himself. It was in writing. I had a legal obligation.

Such a thought. It was foreign, and unwelcome. It felt upsetting. "But God, I want to leave this in Your hands, not mine. So, why are You letting him suffer like this?"

The conversation continued. "I let Dennis decide when he was able. He took it out of My hands when the extra measures were taken: he was put on a ventilator, he had the tracheotomy, he got the feeding tube. I taught him a lot these last months. It was worth it to him."

"But isn't there still a chance that You can heal him, restore him?"

"And if you make a decision to remove the feeding tube, do you think that means I can't restore him, if that's My plan? He asked you to decide for him. I know it's hard, but can you do it? Can you put it back in My hands now?"

It's morning, and looking over our documents about last wishes and health care power of attorney, I am astounded. It is as I had been reminded in the dream. It now seems clear that I would not be betraying Dennis by discontinuing feedings; I would be betraying him by not doing that. I could stop prolonging his suffering and trust the outcome to God.

Simple Does Not Mean Easy

June 3, 2023
Home in Hayward

Am I depressed? Is this too heavy? I have made the decision, and the feeding tube has been removed. All those feelings I've had of hopelessness and being helpless were lies. Dennis had given me the power to change course, and it was simple to do, but hard. I know that it is the best thing for us both. Now, we rest and wait.

Our doctors and the hospice team have been supportive of the decision. It's almost as if they had been wondering when, not if. They seem more concerned about me, wanting me to be certain and not have regrets.

I have decided to be in the moment and look around the space I am in right now. I'm focusing on someone in that space who brings me happiness. I'm letting gratitude for that person overwhelm me and be my reward. And I can feel that being grateful is good for me. It is healing.

Where We're At

June 9, 2023
Home in Hayward

It's spring. Dennis and I are sitting in the living room. I am trying to feed him sips of coffee. He coughs and chokes each time he swallows. He wants to know where Shirley is, his wife. I'm not sure I've convinced him that I'm here. In a voice so soft I can barely catch every other word, he says he has had something he wanted to tell Shirley but she wasn't here. Where did she go?

He says that he got a call from someone telling him that everyone should read the book he's written. It's a book about blood pressure. He wants to know if my mom has read it. While he talks, he is always staring up at the ceiling as if he's connecting with something up there or in another world.

Yesterday's conversation was my attempt to talk with him about death. I asked him if he was afraid to die. There are many questions I ask him that he takes the liberty of not answering—this was one of them. I explained that I was asking because I wanted to remind him there was nothing to fear. Death would be a good change because of what we believe about Jesus's promises. I told him God would probably be in favor of him playing the trumpet again and would give him back his lip control. He would likely be able to walk again, swallow and eat again, and maybe even be with "his dog, Blackie." He would be able to ask all the questions he ever wanted answered. I could tell it sounded good to him, and he repeated some of it with as much excitement as I've seen from him lately. Then, he went to sleep for the rest of the morning.

And he is sleeping again now. It is his default state, to be off in another world where none of these weird things are happening. He rouses only to inquire about new voices he hears in the room—some of them are real, some are in his head only.

I have been reading a book about another man who had Lewy body dementia, written by his caregiver wife. There are so many similarities. That man did not know he had that diagnosis until after he had a stroke. Like Dennis, his disease progressed much faster after the stroke. His time at one hospital after another and finally ending up in a nursing home sounded very familiar to me. I remember pushing Dennis around the halls at Maple Ridge, seeing all the elderly lined up in their chairs around the nursing station with vacant expressions on their faces. It was depressing to him then and he didn't want to look at them, or to be them.

The man in the book felt that same way. I am glad Dennis is not in a nursing home now, although I'm sure they try to be as kind as possible. I feel that I've been able to protect some of his dignity.

Another Change

June 10, 2023
Home in Hayward

Another change, or several changes, really.

There has come a time when we feel we have done all we needed to do, all we could do. There is only the hard waiting left. That's how it is now.

Dennis has shown more signs of discomfort and some frustration, even when he can't explain to us what he is feeling. Sleeping all day, and then sleeping all night, or trying to.

Never being sure of what he's seeing because nothing looks familiar.

Not being sure whether his eyes are open or shut, because either way, things look crazy.

No matter how carefully people move his body, he's left feeling "like a piece of meat."

Being concerned about the meeting he was supposed to have with a client, and then being told that he is retired and doesn't have to worry about work at all.

I can tell he is feeling puzzled when he gets that small wrinkle between his eyes and he stares at the ceiling, trying to figure things out. When asked how he's doing, he most often answers that he is okay.

Now, he has managed to tell me a few times that he is not doing so well.

He listens more than talks. He stays alert for 10 minutes (max) and then has to sleep. He still thinks about food, but says he is not really hungry. His reflexes are diminishing, the usual rigidity is softening. I don't think he will be here much longer. I will miss him, but I will not miss his suffering. I don't think he will miss it either.

What Is It Like?

June 19, 2023
Home in Hayward

What is it like? That is the question most often in my mind as I watch the husband. He lies in his bed looking peaceful, but his breathing takes off at times and his eyes open wide. I wonder if he is actually seeing something other than the ceiling when his eyes are open.

He doesn't seem to be in pain. I wonder, if death doesn't come with pain, what does it come with? How does it feel to the person dying? Sometimes he makes sounds that could indicate pain and that sound like pain signals to me, but then they cease without any treatment.

I remember the vivid dreams he often had that would make him shout and cry out (and punch and kick!). Is that what's happening as his mind lets go? Does he have real memories? Do his dreams mirror reality, or are they even more frightening?

My intuition tells me the end is very close. Close enough that I am hesitant to leave, even for a short while. I want him to feel like there is someone with him as long as he's here. I know he doesn't always know who is with him, but he does act calmer when he's not alone. He knows someone is there.

I have mixed feelings about friends and family who ask if they should come, and that's actually a good thing. The ones who come because they can, or need to for their own reasons. They are welcome and help me feel supported. The ones who can't come, no matter what the reason, are also helping. I am glad they are preserving memories of the husband that are far more dignified, heartwarming, and joyful than the memories I am making now. I'm okay with not having everyone see him go through this.

If I could see his spirit, I'm sure this experience would be different. Unfortunately, what I see is his body, the damaged shell his spirit has to reside in. There is nothing pleasant or easy about watching someone die. In my career as a nurse, I've seen death fairly often. I suppose that helps me some now—at least I am not surprised. But each death is unique, and I've never seen my husband die.

At night, I most often pull the recliner up next to his bed, so I can take his hand when he seems to be agitated. I've gotten used to the signs that mean he needs to change position. I sleep with the sound of his breathing in my ears, either loud and wet or so quiet and shallow that I need to look. Breath and life are so closely allied that the physical action of drawing in air takes in a sacredness. I wonder which one will be his last.

I wonder, I wonder, I wonder... I wonder if he is trying to let go, or struggling not to. I wonder if he's even aware that it is time.

A New Beginning

June 20, 2023
Hayward

Dennis, the husband, died early this morning. The bad thing, the difficult, uncomfortable, discouraging, sad thing is over, and the good that was promised him is beginning. That's the story that both of us have believed, and we're very happy to stick with it. A new beginning for him, made possible by faith in Jesus Christ.

What's uppermost in my mind, as I sit in this empty living room, are the things I believe about God. I love it that God did not want any of His creation to be wasted. I love that He always planned a way for the imperfect to become perfect, and that the way had to be through a relationship with Him. It's a precious thing to feel known, valued, and loved even when I haven't earned it. Even more importantly, nothing on earth can take away or change what God has in mind for me, or what He has in mind for Dennis. I love having the worldview of the One who made the world.

It's a new beginning for me as well. I am a widow. A single, after 50 years of being otherwise. I'm grateful for those years and for being able to spend them with Dennis. There's a lot to process here, and it might take a while. It's called grieving. I'm also aware of a new compassion for people who are facing end-of-life decisions, and suddenly, those people are everywhere.

Memorial

July 28, 2023
Hayward, WI

Memorial services are important in many ways. It's not insignificant that a person has come to the end of earthly life. I felt like this was my last public opportunity to honor the man I knew and loved for fifty years. I wanted those who would come to be reminded of how Dennis spent his time. I wanted them to hear the stories about his accomplishments, his struggles, and his faith. I wanted to remind them about how unique he was, and how grateful I was to have known him. I wanted people to know how content and brave he was in the face of a terrible illness.

At the end of his memorial service, a recording of one of Dennis's favorite songs was played, followed by an audio clip that he left on daughter Esther's phone months before. As we listened to him speak that message to her, it was like hearing him speak from the other side of death.

"Hey, Esther, this is Dad. Can I tell you? About an hour ago, my trumpet *(his ability to play trumpet)* came back! Can you believe it? Now, my lips are tired, they feel tired, but it's not something I've been feeling for a year. And I can play with good tone! Man, it's so much fun to have that trumpet return. You know what I'm talking about! And the whistler is strong *(He whistled a few notes).* Bye"

It was joyful and full of hope, and that is how I will always remember Dennis. Both of us have gone through this very difficult time, but he was the one who faced off with dementia and death. He did it in his own characteristic way, like a researcher, like a scientist, and finally, like a believer in the resurrection. To some, it may look like he lost the fight, but he never voiced that thought. And I expect that his next moments of awareness will be in a better place, where his joy is even more real, all his hopes have been realized, and he can pick up his trumpet and play it any time he wants to.

Epilogue

On July 24, 2023, one month after Dennis's death, a baby girl was born to our daughter and her husband. She is Dennis's only grandchild, and although he did not get to meet her, he did know she was coming. He saw the ultrasound and knew it was "Julie's baby." Perhaps during some of those difficult nights, he was praying for her safe arrival and for the woman she would become.

I think of him leaving and her arriving so close together but never having met. To me, it is a little like God's thoughtfulness, His assurance that life goes on and must be attended to. Babies take time and attention, and this little one certainly helped me to sit comfortably with grief and joy in close proximity. She will continue to be a part of Dennis's story. I know I will probably see something in her, from time to time, that reminds me of him, and that will be sweet.

www.ingramcontent.com/pod-product-compliance
Ingram Content Group UK Ltd.
Pitfield, Milton Keynes, MK11 3LW, UK
UKHW041632190726
13854UKWH00006B/2443